JOHN EVELYN, COOK

Frontispiece: Portrait of John Evelyn by Robert Walker, 1648.

(Photograph by courtesy of the National Portrait Gallery.)

The Rusticall and Œconomical Works of
J O H N   E V E L Y N

Ἡ δὲ μετάνοια αὐτὴ φιλοσοφίας ἀρχὴ γίνεται
REPENTANCE IS THE BEGINNING OF PHILOSOPHY

J O H N   E V E L Y N ,
C o o k

THE MANUSCRIPT RECEIPT BOOK OF JOHN EVELYN

edited by
CHRISTOPHER DRIVER

PROSPECT BOOKS

1997

Published by Prospect Books in 1997,
at Allaleigh House, Blackawton, Totnes, Devon TQ9 7DL

British Library Cataloguing in Publication Data:
A catalogue entry of this book is available from the British Library.

Additional material by Tom Jaine and Aileen Hall.

The description 'Rusticall and Œconomical' derives from Evelyn's own
description of such books in a library catalogue he drafted.

The Greek motto on the title page is Evelyn's own, and is seen in the
portrait by Robert Walker on the front of the jacket and the frontispiece.

ISBN 0 907325 653

Printed by The Cromwell Press, Broughton Gifford, Wiltshire.

Table of Contents

Mary Evelyn, an engraving of the drawing by the French artist R. Nanteuil, 1650.

Introduction

John Evelyn (1620-1706), virtuoso, diarist and author, was the second son of a prosperous gentry family of Wotton in Surrey, whose wealth was founded on the manufacture of gunpowder in Queen Elizabeth's reign. After schooling, university and studies at law, he evaded the dangers of civil war by travel in the Low Countries, Italy and France, returning to this country after the battle of Worcester, having married the daughter of the English ambassador to the French royal court. In the course of a long life, spent largely at his house in Deptford, but finally in possession of the paternal estates at Wotton, he wrote many books, planned and maintained gardens, served as a commissioner for the sick and wounded mariners and prisoners of war in 1664–7 and 1672–4, as a member of the Council for Foreign Plantations 1671–4, and as a commissioner for the Privy Seal 1685–7, as well as filling other minor offices. He was a member, and later secretary, of the Royal Society. He sired seven children, of whom one daughter survived him.

As a founder of the Royal Society, he was the first practical advocate of afforestation in England, the first political campaigner against atmospheric pollution in London, and the first gardener-cook for whom meat was incomplete without a salad. He talks to us as our contemporary from a half-century in which a new generation of scientists and philosophers lived alongside the transformers of taste in food, fashion, drama and music.

His contribution was as interpreter of changes in taste that had occurred in Europe in the years of war and interregnum, particularly in the fields of gardening, architecture and city planning. His pursuits might serve as touchstone to the preoccupations of many of his peers, and he was guide and mentor to many both richer and more powerful than he, from the King downwards. It was Evelyn, for example, who discovered the sculptor Grinling Gibbons and set him on his path to fame. He nurtured an intense Anglican faith, and held a strong moral line through his life, which can be charted from entries in the voluminous diary which has survived.

The manuscripts of John Evelyn reposed for more than forty years in the library of Christ Church, my Oxford college. Some time in the 1950s, I saw exhibited there a large volume bound in decorated calf gilt, with Evelyn's arms on the cover and his woodcut bookplate inside. It was titled, *Receipts Medicinal*, and proved on inspection to contain not only prescriptions for sick cattle and humans, but receipts for the still-room, formulas for preserves and perfumery (many of these in Portuguese), and culinary recipes. Much was ornately written by a professional clerk, but much too was in Evelyn's own hand, or so I surmised, and those of other members of his family circle. On my first sighting the manuscript, I had expressed surprise that some publisher or scholar had not mined this rich hoard, but my tastes were perhaps more catholic than those of Geoffrey Keynes, Evelyn's modern bibliographer, who had written, 'A number of other MSS remain unpublished, and it may be doubted whether any of them will ever be considered worthy of being printed.'[1] From time to time thereafter, with the permission of the college, I tapped into a word-processor the 343 receipts of cookery from the unwieldy folio. Evelyn's neat – but faint – hand always gives me a frisson, as though a friend had planted a great walnut tree three centuries ago.

John Evelyn

A book of cookery is hardly the point from which to embark on its author's life odyssey. Although reflections of his enthusiasms, and reverberations of his actions, will doubtless be felt by the reader, they are weakened by the distance imposed by the economical transmission of practical instruction. Such a book is a coda to life, not the main theme.

John Evelyn was a man who loved knowledge, spent many hours hoarding it, then processing it for dissemination. Therein lay his strength, for he lived through a period of great cultural change in his own country. His habits and unbounded curiosity ensured he would be a participating agent, no mere observer.

His education was a stuttering affair. He was unwilling to expose himself to the rigours of boarding school, which meant Eton, and stayed tied to the apron-strings of his step-grandmother in the Sussex countryside until sent to the Middle Temple and Balliol College at the age of seventeen. While university may have afforded a grounding in the essentials of language, philosophy, music and religion, he was ever 'diverted, with inclinations to newer trifles.' The Middle Temple was of no more utility, though he was of sufficient standing to be elected a comptroller of the student revellers at Christmas 1641, even if he did resign his office to spend a quieter season at home.

At some point in these apprentice years a spark of questing enthusiasm and curiosity was ignited. The diary gives little away – but then it is the most reticent of documents. He talks of confirmation at Oxford as being, 'receiv'd (I feare) ... out of curiosity, rather then with that due preparation and advise which had been requisite ... as I have since deplor'd it,' so even his faith, to be a lodestar, sat lightly on his shoulders. As presages of civil war multiplied, he writes of his avoiding political misfortune more from 'the infinite goodnesse, and mercy of God, then the least providence or discretion of myne owne, who now thought of nothing, but the pursute of Vanity, and the confus'd imaginations of Young men.'

Yet in the summer of that year, July 1641, he travelled 'from this ill face of things at home' to the Low Countries and immediately, as we read his own account, the mental landscape is transformed. He busily notes the buildings, the people, the art, the politics, and even the food and drink. He hunted down the famous printing shops of of Elsevier at Leyden and Plantin at Antwerp, visited gardens, went in search of European scholars such as Daniel Heinsius, 'whom I long'd to see,' and included items such as the lime tree at a convent, 'out of whose stem, neere the roote, issue 5 upright & exceeding tall suckers or boles, the like whereof for evenesse & height I had not observ'd.' No more a vain, imagining youth, rather a man of indefatigable eyes and mind.

His guide and mentor in these early years was most likely Thomas Howard, Earl of Arundel (d. 1646), himself a traveller, art lover and collector, with horizons much broader than England. Already, Evelyn had had his portrait painted by one Henrik van der Borcht, a painter in Arundel's employ; on his tour of the Netherlands, Evelyn fell in with Arundel, who was in Flanders as escort to Queen Henrietta Maria; later, they were to meet again in Italy, where the Earl provided him with 'directions, all written in his owne hand, [of] what curiosities I should enquire after in my journey.' He was never very far from the charmed circle of the Howard family – designing in 1667 the gardens at Albury in Surrey for Henry Howard, Arundel's grandson, later Duke of Norfolk (donor of the Arundel Marbles to Oxford University, at Evelyn's prompting). In 1662 he wrote of a visit to Albury, 'I was much obliged to that great virtuoso [Arundel] and to this young Gent: [Henry Howard] so as I staied a fortnight with him.'

Whoever first directed Evelyn's thoughts and steps towards being the ultimate connoisseur was thorough. One short journey overseas and he was back with his elder brother at the family seat of Wotton in Surrey designing a fishpond, island and 'some other solitudes & retirements, … which gave the first occasion … to those Water-Workes and Gardens, which afterwards succeeded them, and became the most famous in England at that tyme.' A longer trip, from 1643 until 1647, through France and Italy, only returning after marriage to the daughter of Sir Richard Browne, the English ambassador in Paris, and how much more would he achieve?

His travels were not without purpose. He wrote in 1646, once he had settled for some months at Paris, that this was 'the onely time that in my whole life I spent most idly, tempted from my more profitable recesses; but I soone recovered my better resolutions, & fell to my study, & learning of the high-dutch & Spanish tongues, & now & then refreshing my Dauncing, & such exercises as I had long omitted, & which are not in such reputation among the sober Italians.'

*****

In January 1653, John Evelyn 'began to set out the Ovall Garden at Says Court, which was before a rude Orchard, & all the rest one intire field of 100 Ackers, without any hedge: excepting the hither holly-hedge joyning to the bank of the mount walk: & this was the beginning of all the succeeding Gardens, Walkes, Enclosures & Plantations there.' These gardens were to be famous in their own time, though their remains are now but post-holes and shadows on an archaeologist's ground plan.

He 'dug and raild' a carp pond; installed an aviary, where the Marquis of Argyll in 1656 mistook turtle doves for owls; set up a transparent beehive and a house for wild pigeons; planned a garden with 38 beds of potherbs, and plots for melons, peas and beans; planted a line of pearmains and codlins between the Oval Garden and the Grove, as well as 300 fruit trees in the great orchard; and terminated the apple-tree walk by a moated island, filled with asparagus, raspberries and a mulberry tree, and ringed by hedges of fruit: *elysium Britannicum* – paradise.

Sayes Court in Deptford belonged to his father-in-law, Sir Richard Browne. John was not his father's heir-apparent, and suffered the double loss of any younger child on his death in 1640. Often, the Evelyn family looked after its own, in houses that formed part of the Wotton estate, but John, though inheriting land in Sussex, had nowhere to live on his return from France, a married man, in 1647. He did not actually bring his wife – she was no more than thirteen, and was left in the care of her mother.

Casting about for a suitable residence, Sayes Court, then occupied by uncle-in-law Prettyman, seemed a happy solution: close to London, within striking distance of his family scattered along the Surrey hills between Wotton (near Dorking) and Godstone, and the inheritance of the Brownes, whose only daughter, Mary, was Evelyn's child-bride. His being there in the aftermath of the Civil Wars might also ensure its protection from Roundhead depredations. The house itself was no masterpiece – he regretted its modesty – but afforded *tabula rasa* for an experiment in gardening.

Evelyn roomed in the house at the outset, 'I had a lodging, & some books', only converting to purchase in 1653, but then remained in occupation until he inherited Wotton itself on the death of his brother in 1699. This generation was dogged by mortality: Evelyn, his wife Mary and his brother George may have notched up two centuries between them, but siblings, children, and George's wives dropped like flies.

As Evelyn admitted his travels were over, so he built upon and consolidated his accumulated reserves of knowledge and observation. The next fifteen years saw the production of most of his books: translations of French works on politics, gardening, architecture and bibliophily, and of classical poetry and prose; his great treatise on arboriculture, *Sylva*; the *Kalendarium Hortense*; a study of engraving; political tracts; discourses on air pollution and cider-making. Meanwhile he created his own gardens in French mode, and transformed his brother's land at Wotton and Henry Howard's at Albury into something out of Italy. In his library, he gathered materials for his magnum opus, covering every aspect of the gardener's art, *Elysium Britannicum*; made notes on 'secrets and receipts mechanical' for an account of the trades of England; recorded formulas and recipes for medicine and cookery; and fired off innumerable squibs to his friends of the Royal Society. From about the middle of the 1660s, although he never stopped working (he complains of rarely getting to bed before midnight or one o'clock), his energies were consumed in new and different ways. He took active public office for the first time; his children were increasing, both in number and in their burden of care; his literary works were fewer, and less significant, yet his devotional writing (albeit unpublished) was apparently an unstaunchable flow.

John Evelyn is not an easy man to know. His long diary, where notes of sermons become more prolix as years go by, has not the accessibility of his friend's, Samuel Pepys. It is reticent, sometimes almost mendacious by omission, occasionally tiresome. He can seem by turns an insufferable prig, a sycophant, one who carps and complains. Yet testimony survives of his wit and attraction, above all from Pepys, whose judgement in 1665 was, 'in fine, a most excellent person he is, and must be allowed a little for a little conceitedness; but he may well be so, being a man so much above others. He read me, though with too much gusto, some little poems of his own, that were not transcendent.'

There is a certain modesty about Evelyn that is not altogether false. He wrote a letter to Samuel Pepys in 1689 which commented on his friend's request that he sit to the artist Kneller for a portrait to adorn the walls of Pepys's library. Among the Boyles, the Gales, and the Newtons, he protests, 'what, in God's name, should a planter of colewort do?' Pepys and his circle provoked another charming aside. There was a club of like minds that met in Pepys's lodgings in York Buildings and Evelyn suggested his grandson Jack write a florid Latin eulogy, each member to have a short epigram to characterize him. For himself, he suggested, 'gardener and salad-maker' – the year was 1699, when *Acetaria* was finally published.

Evelyn's inward feelings, that the reader may hope to find laid bare in as self-centred a document as a diary, are often inscrutable – or difficult of comprehension to modern sensibility. Not least his friendship during the 1670s with the young maid of honour, Margaret Blagge, later Mrs Godolphin, which veers between religious hysteria and something more confusedly of the flesh. We may detect in that passionate relationship across the altar more of St Theresa of Avila than of Rev. Obadiah Slope, but it does bespeak a certain ambivalence towards pleasure and indulgence. This was mirrored in his advice to his son on the eve of his marriage in 1679: 'Take heed of those filthy lusts even with your own wife, nor delight to feed and satisfy your eyes or incite your fancy with nakedness, or unnatural figures and usages of yourselves, for they will breed impudence, loathing and contempt ... be none of those who brag how frequently they can be brutes in one night.' He was often free with sexual advice: to his wife shortly after their own marriage, and to Margaret Blagge as well, though his precepts to them are now unknown.

Puritanism in his character surfaces repeatedly in strictures on the conduct of the royal court under Charles II, something which may also be picked up from the diary of Samuel Pepys, though his complaints were more about the consequences on the Navy Office of failure of executive nerve through indolent hedonism than the lashings of indignant morality. Pepys may have racked his conscience for inattention or unfaithfulness, indeed his whole career seems founded on the triumph of will over desire, but he did at least indulge himself. Evelyn's lapses appear less frequent and full-blooded, though he evidently was no stranger to enjoyment – highbrow might be one epithet. And towards the end of his life, he was almost an ascetic. In 1695 he was abstaining from breakfast and supper, to the evident concern of his wife: 'some liquid suppings of gruel or milk, tea, or syrup of violets with water and some drops of sulphur might help in the morning … as long before dinner as you can,' she wrote. While his behaviour may have been the result of either conscious thought or natural disposition, he was also witness to the terrible effects of over-indulgence. His nephew drank himself to repeated stupors and an early grave, and his own son, John, ran perilously close to a similar fate – at a time the family fortunes could hardly afford it. 'You offend,' wrote an outraged father, 'and forget your duties, … your consuming an whole night with an insipid sot, heat your blood and disorder your health, in the boast of being able to contain more drink than another, making your body a tun.'

There are other signs of Evelyn's possible disapproval of food, or certainly of the Rabelaisian approach to eating. In 1685, when he had lost his favourite daughter to the smallpox, he wrote to her sister warning her against 'trash and sweetmeats which have chiefly been the cause of Mary's death. She eat those filthy things so constantly at My lady Falkland's that it was impossible to overcome the tough phlegm they had bread in her.' Some years before that, when Margaret Godolphin was setting up house, she reported – sure that such conduct would gain her mentor's approval – 'As to our family, … three dishes of meat at dinner we would willingly have, and no suppers at all.'

An almost religious asceticism can be seen in Evelyn's proposal to Robert Boyle for a monkish college as the core of the future Royal Society. In Carthusian style, acolytes or scholars were to have their own cells, and follow a rigorous timetable. John and Mary were to be the resident wardens, living in separate cells, 'for we are to be decently asunder'. Not much shrift was given to food: 'an old woman to dress the meat … one meal a day, of two dishes only (unless some little extraordinary upon particular days or occasions, never exceeding three) of plain and wholesome meat; a small refection at night…'

These attitudes have relevance because the manuscript on display in this book is a collection of cookery recipes, a form we often associate with pleasure, excessive or not. In making it, was John Evelyn impelled by hedonism, more balanced epicureanism (he did translate Lucretius), a

desire to record past and present techniques and practices, a wish for true
economy, or a search for better health in mind and body?

We seek in vain in Evelyn's diary for expressions of happy greed and
satisfaction such as constantly recur in the daily record of Samuel Pepys
or, later, Parson James Woodforde. In part this derives from Evelyn's
method of writing. Pepys and Woodforde wrote journals, on or about the
day in question. Small wonder, therefore, that food bulks large – either its
consumption, digestion or preparation. Evelyn's diary was written at greater
distance. He may have made rough jottings, but much was composed
retrospectively. As Ponsonby remarked, it is nearer autobiography than
diary.[2] Recording the minutiae of daily cooking was bound to suffer,
especially if, as we have already noted, there was an element in his character
that steered him away from such things.

Food is allowed a place in the record when it was curious, reflecting on
a particular place, or on the habits of strange people. Mention of it also
occurs more often in the earlier, travelling, accounts, than when he was
finally settled in his own home. What is almost entirely lacking, is any
detail about what he ate from day to day, or even during visits to grand
houses and families.

The following paragraphs contain the more interesting references to
food in the diary; there is another handful of no interest at all. (I have used
the texts established by de Beer, or the later editor Guy de la Bédoyère,
giving date rather than page, so that items may be more quickly found in
other, more accessible, editions.)

30 September, 1644.
[In Vienne, France] ... here were the first Truffles or Earth-nuts I had eaten
before found in the field: by a nasute hog, trained up to it.

31 January, 1645.
[In Italy] ... the most pleasant Plaines of Campania, now call'd Terra di
Lavoro: In very truth I thinke the most fertile spot, that ever the Sunn shone
upon. ... 'tis commonly reported one Vine will loade 5 mules with its Grapes:
but what much adds to the pleasure of these rusticities is that the Vines climbing

to the summit of the trees reach in festoons & fruitages from one tree to another, planted at exact distances, which shewing like a greene Chayne about a field, is pleasanter than any painting can describe it: there likewise growes Rice, Canes for Suggar, Olives, Pomegranads, Mulberrys, Cittrons, Oranges, Figgs and infinite sorts of rare fruits. ... About noone We enter'd the Citty of Naples, allighting at the 3 Kings, a Place of treatment to excesse, as we found by our very plentifull fare all the tyme we were in Naples, where provisions are miraculously cheape, & we seldome sat downe to fewer than 18 or 20 dishes of the most exquisite meate & fruites.

May, 1645.

[Bologna, Italy] This Citty is famous also for sausages; and here is sold great quantities of Parmegiano cheese, with Botargo, Caviare &c which makes some of their shops perfume the streets, with no agreeable smell.

June, 1645.

[Venice] I had now resolved to imbarke myselfe, intending to see Jerusalem ... I was provided of all necessaries, laied in Snow to coole our drink, bought some Sheepe, Poultry, Bisquit, Spirits & a little Cabinet of Drouggs ...

July/August, 1645.

[Murano, Venice] In this place are excellent oysters, small and well tasted like our Colchester, and they were the first, as I remember, that I ever could eate, for I had naturally an aversion to them.

22 October, 1650.

[In Paris] I din'd at my Lord Stanhop where we drank too liberaly. [See his receipt for seasoning cherries, 102, below.]

27 June, 1654.

[At Bristol] Here I first saw the manner of refining Suggar, & casting it into loaves, where we had a collation of Eggs fried in the suggar furnace, together with excellent Spanish wine.

22 July, 1654.

[In Wiltshire] We departed & dined at a ferme of my U. Hungerfords ... most sweetly water'd, abounding in Trowts and all things else requisite, provision exceeding cheape: They catch the Trouts by Speare in the night, whilst they come wondring at a light set in the sterne: There were Pigeons, Conys, & foule in aboundance, & so we had an excellent dinner at an houres warning ...

8 July, 1656.

[Colchester] For the rest, this is a raged, factious Towne, and now swarming in Sectaries. ... It is also famous for Oysters, & Erringo of rootes here about growing & Candied.

16 January, 1662.

After this I accompanied the Duke to an East India vessel that lay at Black-Wall, where he had Entertain[me]nt of several curiosities; among other spirituous drinks, as Punch &c, they gave us Canarie that had ben carried to & brought back from the Indies, which was indeede incomparably good.

30 November, 1662.

... was the first Anniversary our Society for the Choice of new Officers. ... after the Election was over we all dined together his Majesty sending us Venison.

22 May, 1666.

... din'd with my L: Cornbury now made L. Chamberlaine to the Queene, who kept a very honourable table, & so home.

19 August, 1668.

[At the reception of the French ambassador Colbert by the King Charles II] There was of that rare fruite called the King-Pine, ... the first of them I had ever seen; His Majestie having cut it up, was pleased to give me a piece off his owne plate to tast of, but in my opinion it falls short of those ravishing varieties of deliciousnesse, ... but possibly it might be (& certainly was) much impaired in coming so farr: It has yet a gratefull accidity, but tasts more of the Quince and Melon.

3 July, 1679.

[In the Tower of London] Sending a piece of Venison to Mr Pepys Sec: of the Admiralty, still a Prisoner, I went and dined with him.

4 December,1679.

I dined ... at the Portugal Ambassadors now new come, at Cleaveland house ... the Entertainement was exceeding Civile, but besids a good *olio*, the dishes were trifling, hash'd & Condited after their way, not at all fit for an English stomac, which is for solid meate: There was yet good fowl but roasted to Coale; nor were the sweetemeates good.

26 April, 1681.

I dined with Dom Piedro Ronquillos the Spanish Ambassador at Wild House, used me with extraordinary Civility: After dinner (which was plentifull, halfe after the Spanish, & halfe after the English way) ...

24 August, 1681.

I was invited to Mr. Denzil Onslows at his seate at Purford, where was much company & such an extraordinary feast. as I had hardly ever seene at any Country Gent: table in my whole life; but what made it more remarkable was, that there was not any thing, save what his Estate about it did not afford; as Venison, Rabbits, hairs, Pheasants, Partridge, [pigeons,] Quaile, Poultrie, all sorts of fowle in season (from his owne Decoy neere his house) all sorts of fresh fish: so Industrious is this worthy Gent: After dinner we went to see sport at the decoy, I never saw so many herons &c.

24 January, 1682.

... I was at the Entertainement of the Morrocco (Ambassador) at the Dut: of Portsmouth's glorious Appartment at W:hall, where was a greate banquet of Sweetemeates, & Musique & but at which both the Ambassador & Retinue behaved with extraordinary Moderation & modestie, though placed about a long Table a Lady between two Moores: viz a Moore, then a Woman, then a Moore, & and most of these were the Kings natural Children, viz.: the Lady Lichfield, Sussex, DD of Portsmouth, Nelly &c.: Concubines, & catell of that sort as splendid as Jewells, and Excesse of Bravery could make them: the Moores neither admiring or seeming to reguard any thing, furniture or the like with any earnestnesse; and but decently tasting of the banquet: They dranke a little of Milk & Water, but not a drop of Wine, also they drank of a sorbett & Jacolatte.

20 June, 1682.

[At the reception for the ambassadors of Bantam, in Java, at Lord George Berkeley's] Their meate was cook'd, carried up, & they attended on, by severall fat Slaves, who had no Covering save drawes, their whole body from the girdle upward stark naked, as well as their leggs, which appeared very uncouth, & lothsom; They eate their *pilaw* & other spoone-meate without spoones, taking up their pottage in the hollow of their fingers, & very dextrously flung it into their mouthes, without spilling a drop:

18

22 October, 1685.

[Swallowfield, Berkshire, Lord Clarendon's house] ... the house is after the antient building of honourble gent: houses where they kept up the antient hospitality: But the Gardens & Waters as elegant as 'tis possible to make a flat, with art & Industryie and no means Expenses, my Lady being so extraodinary skill'd in the flowry part: & the dilligence of my Lord in the planting: so that I have hardly seene a seate which shews more toakens of it, then what is here to be found, not onely in the delicious & rarest fruits of a Garden, but in those innumerable & plentifull furniture of the grounds about the seate of timber trees to the incredible ornament & benefit of the place:

There is one Ortchard of a 1000 Golden & other cider Pepins: Walks & groves of Elms, Limes, Oake: & other trees: & the Garden so beset with all manner of sweete shrubs, as perfumes the aire marvelously: The distribution also of the Quarters, Walks, Parterre &c is excellent: The Nurseries, Kitchin-garden, full of the most desireable plants; two very noble Orangeries well furnish'd; but above all, the Canale, & Fishponds, the one fed with a white, the other with a black-running water, fed by a swift & quick river; so well & plentifully stor'd with fish, that for Pike, Carp, Breame & Tench; I had never seene any thing approching it: we had Carps & Pike &c of size fit for the table of a Prince, every meale, & what added to the delight, the seeing hundreds taken in the drag, out of which the Cooke standing by, we pointed what we had most mind to, & had Carps every meale, that had ben worth at London twenty shill a piece: the Water are all flag'd about with *Calamus arromaticus*; of which my Lady has hung a Closset, that retaines the smell very perfectly.

27 October, 1685.

I was invited to Sir St: Foxes, with my L. Lieutenant, where was such a dinner for variety of all things I had seldom seene & it was so, for the triall of a Master-Cooke, which Sir Stephen had recommended to go with his Lordship into Ireland: there was all the Dainties not onely of the season; but of what art could add: Venison, & plain solid Meate, Fowle, Baked & boiled meates; banquet & in exceedingly plenty, & exquisitely dressed.

18 December, 1685.

[At the reception of the Venetian ambassadors by the King] The banquet [i.e. the course of sweetmeats served after and apart from the dinner itself] was 12 vast Chargers pild up so high, as those who sat one against another could hardly see one another, of these Sweetemeates which doubtless were some dayes piling up in that exquisite manner, the Ambassadors touched not, but leaving them to the Spectators who came in Curiosity to see the dinner, &c were exceedingly pleas'd to see in what a moment of time, all that curious work was demolish'd, & the Comfitures &c voided & table clear'd.

These are the notes of a geographer, ethnologist or topographer. Few relate to pleasure. That which is most obviously enthusiastic is the near ecstatic description of Lord Clarendon's estate – and Evelyn's receipts have their fair share of carp and pike. The progression from an interest in growing things (doubtless Evelyn's most persistent hobby-horse) to cooking and eating them is often short. Published writers of the era who fit that bill include Sir Hugh Plat and Gervase Markham; after Evelyn's death there was another distinguished example in Richard Bradley FRS.

Mary Evelyn (c. 1635–1709)

Two quotations: the first from John's *Legend of the Pearl*, never published; the second part of a letter that Mary Evelyn wrote to John when she was in London during the year 1701 and he remained behind at Wotton.

'The prettyness and innocence of her youth had something methought in her that pleased me in a gravity I had not observed in so tender a bud: for I could calle her woman for nothing, but her early steadiness, and that at the age of playing with babies, she would be at her book, her needle, drawing of pictures, casting accompts and understood to govern the house … she began to discourse not impertinently, was gay enough for my humour; and one I believed that might one day grow up to be the agreeable companion of an honest man: … I made this creature my wife, and found a pearl…. [She made] the best wife in the world, sweet and (though not charming) agreeable, and as she grew up, pious, loyal, and of so just a temper, obliging and withall discreet, as has made me very happy.'

'I hope you do not spare any of the good things I left in the closet for your use. When the next hog is killed, the butcher should cut a little more flesh to the chine, and not chop off the hog's snout from the head. I shall be glad Margaret should send some part of the sauce when she sends the hog puddings, spare rib and chine. Let the gardener know the apples were very well packed and kept from bruising, but he laid too much hay between the rows so that we have fewer apples than he might have sent. I would not have him send any of the apples which were bought; they being gathered before the time have little taste; they were better spent at home in apple pies mixed with the others.'

Mary Evelyn was clearly a remarkable woman. She would repay greater study than has yet been given her, for much of her correspondence has survived.

She married at an indecently young age, perhaps twelve, no more than fourteen. John Evelyn was evidently attracted to the younger woman: first his wife, then his other passion, Margaret Blagge, who was sixteen when first taken up by him – he was forty-eight. Perhaps he felt more at ease in their company, more able to dominate, as he was to be an overbearing, though loving, father to his children. He once wrote of his reputation at court, 'some said I was morose, and affected, others that I was plainly stupid, and a fop.' He needed security to fully vent his personality.

Once married in 1647, Mary was left in the hands of her parents in Paris while John returned to England, sending her none the less his *Instructions œconomique*: a blow-by-blow account of housewifery, sexual conduct and deportment. Cohabitation did not begin until the autumn of 1649 on his gaining Paris once more. There is an entry in the diary for September that they took Holy Communion together for the first time. In May of 1651 she miscarried her first child, aged perhaps sixteen, 'proceeding from some Physick prescribd, not believing she was with Child:' A year later, she nearly repeated the harrowing experience: 'I must confess I was never more surprised … after all that physic and letting blood, which was enough to have destroyed it,' she reported from Paris as she embarked on a hazardous journey towards Deptford, pausing at Tunbridge Wells to give birth to her eldest son, who died aged six. She bore seven children in all, four boys and three girls. Only the youngest daughter survived her.

The young bride, now mother, was to endure further misfortune with the loss to scarlet fever of her own mother in the same year, as the new family was setting out to visit long-missed relations. Fortitude in the face of mortality was to be her lot. Evelyn's assessment of her character, quoted above, does not seem, on the surface, far wrong. Her presentation at court soon after the Restoration was not a success: 'sweet and (though not charming) agreeable,' he said; perhaps better suited to life at Sayes Court.

She lacked neither spirit nor intellect. She displayed both during his platonic dalliance with Margaret Blagge, and the prolonged absences that this, and royal business, entailed. 'I hope you do not imagine though I live in the country and converse with sea nymphs, now and then with a tarpaulin hero [i.e. sea captains from the dockyard at Deptford], that I do not apprehend the difference between this kind of felicity and that which you possess in a glorious Court,' she wrote to her husband at Christmas in 1672.

Some recompense may have come from her own friendships, with men as well as women, though misconduct has never been alleged. Three men were especially steadfast. Ralph Bohun, tutor to her son, and later vicar of Wotton; Sir Samuel Tuke, the dramatist, and a relation; and the widowed husband of John Evelyn's sister Jane, William Glanville, perhaps the most steadfast, and nearly passionate. It is no coincidence, perhaps, that her friendships were strongest during the Blagge interlude, but letters written then show her again to be a woman of spirit and sense.

'The flowers and greens … are candying in snow to be preserved for the spring, and our delights confined to the little wooden room, which could your perspective reach would for variety be no unpleasing diversion, than to see a dull fire, circled with a philosopher [Bohun], a woman, and a child, heaps of books, our food, and entertainment, silence our law so strictly observed that neither dog nor cat dares transgress it, the crackling of ice, and whistling winds our music which if continued long in the same quarter may possibly freeze our wits as well as our pens.'

This was to Samuel Tuke, in 1669. Letters from Glanville make it clear she would have been a fine catch for anyone, and a letter to Ralph Bohun in 1675 catches a glimpse of family life: 'amid the groans of Sir Richard

Browne with an attack of the gout (with an addition of pain which leaves us doubtful whether stone or wind) the interruptions of my daughters, the noise of a hammer in the next room and my father's complaints', but her 'success in the oven was not ill, so that we were very merry at the eating of it [a venison pasty], two of the company soaked over a pipe and bottle till eleven at night with great contentment, your company being only wanting.'

Her management of the kitchen was evidently skilful. Letters show detailed knowledge, not mere order-giving. William Glanville praises her cookery. Her skill is again in evidence during the long-running discord between John Evelyn and Lady Mary Wyche his niece, who was never reconciled to the permanent alienation of Wotton from her side of family to John's when the male line failed his brother George, her father, with the death of his eldest son, George junior, in 1676. Lady Wyche kept house at Wotton towards the end of her father's life and in those last years there was constant quarreling fomented by 'the character of her pride, vanity, trifling her time, covetousness, want of housewifery,' so Evelyn thought, at least. Mary could quiet the greatest storm – by cooking. She made a cake so good that even Lady Wyche declared it 'the best she ever eat'. Prophetically, Mary had commented to John ten years before, when travelling down to Bath, 'I find discreet hospitality assists very much towards governing the nation, for common people are led by the mouth with moderate management, and without a little popularity they are perfect mules and ungovernable.'

One would wish to know more about Mary. Although it is clear the recipes that are gathered in this manuscript owe at least their beginnings to John's energy, it is hard to imagine that he supplied too much practical help in the production of food. In the list of that part of his library devoted to gardening and other practical matters, printed by Geoffrey Keynes, two books of receipts, among the scores on plants and visual matters, may be noted: Hugh Plat's *Jewel House of Art and Nature* of 1594 in the 1653 edition, and *The Ladies Cabinet Enlarged and Opened: containing many rare secrets and rich ornaments of several kinds* which appeared in 1654

23

over the name of Lord Ruthven. The dates may be significant: the young couple were feeling their way in the art of housekeeping, but for all that the impression is that John kept to his books, and Mary to her cakes – no matter how literate was each party in the other's specialisation. In 1701, when finally installed at Wotton (and Mary was by this time 65 years old), she reported, 'the dairy answers beyond expectation … I shall be glad to have a stillhouse.'

The manuscript

The volume of receipts collected by John Evelyn is doubly remarkable. First, there is specific reference in correspondence to its inception, and, secondly, Evelyn was himself to publish a book about food, specifically about salads, *Acetaria*, in 1699. The manuscript book of receipts contains many also included in *Acetaria*. While scholars of literature or science have long been used to studying the transition from initial draft to printed text, this has not been possible in the field of cookery because manuscript versions of printed books have not survived. How much would one give to see the first version of Hannah Glasse in the author's own hand?

At the beginning of 1649, John Evelyn was in England while his wife was shut up in a Paris besieged by the Prince de Condé. He had a lodging at Sayes Court while looking for a permanent dwelling; he was gathering together all those purchases and collections he made during his travels in France and Italy ('My Wyfe's Unkle … being rob'd by sea of the Dynkirk Pyrats, I lost … my Wife's Picture painted by Monsieur Bourdon'); and he was still studying: 'I went through a Course of Chymistrie at S[ayes] Court.' He had also come across a servant of Sir Richard Browne's who had been left behind in Deptford, and who had latterly migrated towards John Evelyn's brother Richard, who was living at Woodcote Park near Epsom. His name was Richard Hoare, he had only one eye, so dubbed 'the one-eyed Hoare' by his employer, and was an able, if non-professional, calligrapher and scribe. Evelyn called him 'an incomparable writer of severall hands.' He was also a sot, and it was probably drunkenness that finished his relationship with Evelyn four years later.

Hoare was providential. Since 1642 Evelyn had been observing, taking notes, and buying books, pictures and such miscellanea as 'Tables of Veines & Arteries, which I ... caused to be drawne out of several human bodies at Padua.' 'I shall now have time to reduce my studies into a method, for which end his assistance will much ease and please me,' he wrote to Sir Richard. Hoare, who accompanied Evelyn back to Paris after King Charles's execution, was to act as general clerk in matters bibliophilic, dealing with bookbinders and the like, as well as writing furiously.

The reduction of Evelyn's studies to a method took several forms, one of which is the manuscript under discussion: a collection of receipts within a single volume that spanned the disciplines of still-room, kitchen and doctor's surgery. Just such a triptych was created in many other MS collections of the time, as indeed was the book *The Ladies Cabinet Enlarged and Opened* by Lord Ruthven that was on Evelyn's own shelves. Other notes were being schematized at the same time: on gardening and on trades for instance. Early in this process, Evelyn's sister Jane (who died in 1652) wrote a supportive letter agreeing it was 'a pity not to propagate' the receipts 'of our good grandmother.'

Manuscript compilations of recipes have been discussed by several scholars.[3] The seventeenth-century collection by Rebecca Price is a nice comparison.[4] In 1681, Rebecca, a rich London draper's daughter whose family had migrated to the hillocks of Buckinghamshire, was 21 years old and unmarried. Wedlock came two years later, and to be prepared, she compiled two leather-bound folio volumes, one of surgery and physick, the other of cookery and preserves. These she held fast, even unto death, when she willed them to her daughter Alice.

Rebecca Price was not alone in laying this solid foundation of knowledge to her trousseau. One can almost hear across the years the frenzied scribbling of hundreds of nubile quills on freshly ruled pages. The consequence was the preservation, sometimes through generations, of old-fashioned recipes. The inexperienced spinster prepares to fair-copy receipts. She draws off the kitchen shelf her mother's collection; she asks her aunts and grandmothers for their contributions. In a trice, she has bundles from the previous generation – and the one before that, and so on, and on. In the course of life, she jots down new instructions, culled from books, visitors, and dinners-out, and inserts them in her trusty volume – but this time not in fair or tidy hand. Her daughter or grand-daughter then trawls for her own collection. Thus is created another many-layered recipe book, reflecting the habits of centuries.

The process may be seen in the Evelyn manuscript. There are ancient recipes, for example Lady Browne's pudding of entrails (number 40), or Wotton ale (number 128), and there are relative novelties that may reflect up-to-the-minute French practice, for instance that which tells how to stew a chicken or turkey the French way (number 318). There are those which come from the close family circle, and others which are travellers' tales, brought to Evelyn's attention by people like Sir Arthur Hopton, the ambassador in Madrid. It is a thorough mixture, but one that was proved in the cooking and eating, as evidenced by such comments as 'very good', 'there is a much better reciet in the book' (number 145, for a collar of beef, suggesting that Receipt 316 should now supersede this one), or 'if it had been given right which upon triall dos not answer' (the comment about Mrs Black[wood?]'s receipt for a 'very good cake', number 146), and nicest of all, 'almond butter the best way as it was judged by thos who gave the reciet, but upon triall the tast is the best judge' (number 155).

Richard Hoare was the scribe for the first 127 receipts; thereafter hands multiply, and are difficult to ascribe with certainty. An argument, based on similarities in the formation of the capital letter 'T' and general characteristics, can be advanced for much being in John Evelyn's own holograph, and such an elaborate volume hardly lived outside the library for day-to-day jottings or additions. Whoever did the writing, the important fact is that much was actively copied, rather than written out of the head of the scribe. This may account for the many variations in spelling, and certain evident copying errors. It is interesting to observe how many of the receipts for salads and pickles were cleaned up and clarified before insertion into *Acetaria*.

The expectation with most manuscript recipe collections is that their creators were female. The Evelyn volume was not of this group. I have mentioned some aspects of John Evelyn's own character that may have contributed to this fact – his lifelong desire to fire off practical and theoretical instruction to his dependants and his interest in practical minutiae – but it also accords with a certain culinary dilettantism (to repeat the historian Stephen Mennell[5]) among males of the era. Sir Kenelm Digby is the clearest parallel.[6] Lord Ruthven, cited above, is another. The obvious model is French, the prime cultural influence on royalist England. Mennell gives instances from the eighteenth century, but it was a tendency already established. Reading the memoir of the cook and author Robert May, one has the strong impression of noble employers engaged by the production of the kitchen.[7] Digby's book, published posthumously by his steward, typifies the mania for collecting from one's aristocratic acquaintance.

It is in the nature of recipe ascriptions that they afford ground more for speculation than for certitude. When Evelyn notes that such and such was by courtesy of Lord Berkeley, how can we be sure which Lord Berkeley was meant? Not only is there ambiguity even among Evelyn's own acquaintance, depending on the exact year the recipe was obtained, but it may even be the case that the ascription to an individual was made by a previous generation, or is taken from a printed book that has not been identified. Any suggestions as to identity have to be treated with these reservations.

A list of the donors or sources of receipts is given below. Biographical information is contained in notes to the receipts in the manuscript itself, and further references may be gained from the index. The spelling of names is modernised, not left as in the original.

Lady Ashley: this may be a wife of Lord Ashley, later the Earl of Shaftesbury. There was once a proposal that her stepson marry a niece of John Evelyn, which came to nothing.

Lord Bedford: no evident point of contact exists between John or Mary Evelyn and the family of the Earls or Duke of Bedford. Nor does the receipt (number 198), for a rather north-country oatcake, lend a hand.

L[ord] Berkeley: the note may equally apply to a Lady Berkeley, for John

Evelyn was very close to both, acting as Lord Berkeley's agent during his embassy to France in 1676. Lady Berkeley was Margaret Blagge's chaperone.

Mrs Bindy: this person has not been identified.

Mrs Black[wood?]: the reading of this name is in doubt, and the identity behind it has not been established. Hers was the infamous fruit cake that did not work (number 146).

Lady Browne: was Mary Evelyn's mother.

Lady Burton: a cousin of Mary Evelyn's, the daughter of Sir John Prettyman. She married first Sir Thomas Burton of Stockerston in Leicestershire, then Sir William Halford.

Lord Chesterfield: as Lord Stanhope, a friend from days in Paris (a witness to JE's will at that time) and one with whom Evelyn maintained good relations.

Lady Clayton: the wife of an impossibly rich Lord Mayor of London, they were neighbours of the Evelyns, and bought land belonging to John's cousin. Evelyn evidently approved of her accomplishments.

Mrs Clutterbuck: Lady Burton's (above) daughter-in-law was a Clutterbuck.

Lady Cotton: this is probably George Evelyn's (John's elder brother) second wife. She was the widow of Sir John Cotton, and Evelyn invariably referred to her as Lady Cotton, even after remarriage.

A Dane: the identity of this man is shrouded in mystery.

Lady Evelyn: the wife of JE's cousin, Sir John Evelyn, was called Thomasine.

Lady Fitzhardinge: one Lady Fitzhardinge was a Godolphin, and the blessed Margaret Blagge married Sidney Godolphin. This may perhaps be the link.

Lady Glanville: although Evelyn's sister Jane married into the Glanville family, they bore no title, and the most likely identity of this reference is Winifred, the wife of Sir John Glanville, speaker of the Short Parliament, who was Mary Evelyn's uncle and with whom they were on good terms.

Lady Grey: it is impossible to determine whom this refers to. Possibly it was a member of the Grey family, the earls of Kent. There was a distant family connection with the Evelyns and they do crop up in the diary.

Lady Harrington: a doubtful identification; Evelyn seems to be been intimate with no family of this name, although he was acquainted with, and had visited, the Haringtons of Swakeley.

Lady Hatton: there was long-term acquaintance between the Brownes, John Evelyn and Lord and Lady Hatton, stemming from joint residence in Paris. The Evelyns also visited them on their tour of England in 1654. However, there was another Hatton family more closely related to John Evelyn, with whom he was intimate in his youth. The problem is that they bore no title.

Henrietta Maria: there are two receipts ascribed to the Queen. They have not been tied to any printed source, the most obvious being the trilogy *The Queen's Closet Opened* (1655).

Sir Arthur Hopton: this diplomatist provided Evelyn with three Spanish recipes, and a meeting with him is recorded in the diary for 1649 with evident pleasure. There was a further link in that Hopton was a friend of the Earl of Arundel whom he helped in purchasing works of art in Europe.

Lady Huet: the identity of this lady is discussed in the footnote to Receipt 285. The double Evelyn connection to the Mordaunts and the Onslows, replicating the search for Lady 'Hewit' by the modern editor of the eighteenth-century author Martha Bradley who uses her receipts extensively, is too great a coincidence to be ignored.

Lady Mordaunt: John was an executor of Viscountess Mordaunt (d. 1679) and had long been friends with her.

Mrs E. Packer: the reading of this name is doubtful. It is suggested it may be a member of the family of John Evelyn's close friend Philip Packer of Groombridge in Kent.

Lord St Albans: a distinguished courtier with whom Evelyn was hardly on intimate terms, though he was flattered by his attention. Digby also has a receipt from St Albans, and he was obviously a man who enjoyed life.

Lady Shaen: Evelyn was on dining terms with Sir James Shaen FRS and his wife Frances, who was a daughter of the Earl of Kildare. There was a residual connection by marriage between her family and the Brownes which meant that Evelyn could claim kinship with them.

Henry Slingsby: Master of the Royal Mint (Evelyn was on a commission for its regulation in 1663–4, and it was he who proposed the inscription *DECUS &* *TUTAMEN*, which has since girded modern £1 coins, as a device against coin clippers), and colleague on the Council for Foreign Plantations. Slingsby was a fine musician and friend of Samuel Pepys.

Sir Edward Stowell: a friend or acquaintance from Paris days, but no other connection has been discovered.

Mrs Tinker: the identity of this lady is in doubt. There was a maritime neighbour, Captain Tinker, in Deptford. Perhaps, when Mary Evelyn wrote of 'tarpaulin heroes', he was one of them.

Lady Tuke: one of the two wives of Sir Samuel Tuke the playwright, a relative of Mary Evelyn's, and an admirer. His first was Mary Guldeford, d. 1666, kinswoman of Lord Arundell of Wardour. They spent their wedding night at Evelyn's house in 1664. His second was Mary Sheldon (d. 1705).

Marquess of Winchester: there is no obvious connection between the Evelyns and the source of Receipt 1. John writes of meeting Lord Winchester when he visited Lord Montague in 1649, but it is surprising that conversation turned to the best way to make wormwood ale.

Sir Christopher Wren: the architect. Evelyn had long been an admirer, since first meeting him in Oxford, although there is little sign that they were especially intimate. Geoffrey Keynes discovered, in the course of compiling his bibliography, a presentation copy of *Acetaria* inscribed to Wren by Evelyn. The inscription included recipes for carrots and cucumbers: perhaps the gooseberry wine, Receipt 339 below, was fair exchange.

Eighteen of this list might definitely be thought friends or contacts of John Evelyn himself; six can be identified as members of Mary's family or, at least, relations.

The text

The manuscript is contained within a folio volume of 172 folios entitled *Receipts Medicinal*. The volume was divided into five books: (i) 'Receipts Medicinal', 41 folios; (ii) 'Receipts Chirurgical', 17 folios, also containing 'An Addition of Receits for Preserving, March 1695' written in neat italic hand; (iii) 'Receipts of Preserves', with 'and Perfumes' added to the heading in a different hand, 27 folios, on the obverse of several folios the receipts are written in Portuguese; (iiii) 'Receipts of Cookery', 37 folios; (v) 'Receipts for Cattle &c', 2 folios.

Folios 165–172 are a table of contents by category, with careful cross-reference from one book to the other. Although the initial calligraphic work was undertaken by the clerk Richard Hoare, John Evelyn's hand is seen in every section, including the index. The apparent contribution by a later compiler, evinced by the additional heading to book ii, is unexplained.

The present transcription comprises those culinary receipts from book iiii contained within a numbered sequence 1–343. There are some later unnumbered additions which have not been included, and there are a few receipts from the main sequence, specifically for drinks, which have not been printed here. It will be clear that there is still much work to be done, not only on this volume for the light it sheds on seventeenth-century practice in the still-room, but also in the Evelyn MSS in general for additional information about food and cookery within the households of Wotton and Sayes Court.

The transcription deviates as little as possible from the manuscript original. A consistent modern intervention has been to standardise the heading to each receipt. In the MS, the headings are in the margin, often without punctuation, and the receipt numbers are placed centrally at the start of the receipt. Punctuation and spelling in the manuscript are wayward and inconsistent. Richard Hoare supplied much punctuation; later receipts are almost entirely devoid of it. The present transcription has not modernized the spelling, and has rarely supplied letters (and then invariably within square brackets) to make words more familiar. When the editorial intervention is constant and consistent, for instance in extending 'p' to 'p[ound]' (always in square brackets), no footnote is written, but where there may be doubt, a footnote records any editorial changes, by stating that a particular alteration is supplied. One defence of this line is that variations in spelling give some clue about the provenance, age, or authorship of a particular recipe or group of entries. The major exception is that where the manuscript has the letter 'u' where we would now write 'v', the modern spelling has been preferred. Neither punctuation nor regular capitalization has been supplied, except a final full stop to each paragraph (again within square brackets). This makes recipes difficult to untangle, but is preferable to offering a sanitized version.

Many questions of language and terminology have been addressed in the footnotes, especially where they pertain to a single occurrence. Wider questions, or things which may occur in more than one place, are discussed in the glossary. The index provides a concordance, and has been compiled to record mentions of most ingredients.

A note on sources and acknowledgements

Details of books consulted are in the bibliography below. The introduction was composed relying entirely on printed sources, in particular W.G. Hiscock and E.S. de Beer. There is untapped wealth still contained in the manuscripts which it must be hoped will soon result in new perceptions of John Evelyn and his family as the papers are catalogued and made available in the British Library.

I am most grateful to the Librarian of Christ Church for access to the manuscripts in the first instance and to Dr Frances Harris of the Department of Manuscripts, the British Library. The staffs of the National Portrait Gallery and the London Library have been of great assistance. Stewart Kelly helped check the transcription, and Jane Stevenson came to the rescue on matters palaeographic at very short notice. Pat Phillips kindly helped translate one of the receipts from the French, and John Harrison translated the recipe for bondejo from the Spanish.

References in the introduction.

[1] Geoffrey Keynes, *John Evelyn, a Study in Bibliophily*, Cambridge 1937, p. 243.

[2] Arthur Ponsonby, *English Diaries from the XVIth to the XXth Century*, London 1923, pp. 97-8.

[3] e.g. C. Anne Wilson, ed., *Traditional Country House Cooking*, London 1993; Karen Hess, *Martha Washington's Booke of Cookery*, New York 1981; Edith Hörandner, 'The Recipe Book as a Cultural and Socio-historical Document', *Food in Perspective*, eds. A. Fenton & T.M. Owen, Edinburgh 1981.

[4] Madeleine Masson, int., *The Compleat Cook*, London 1974.

[5] Stephen Mennell, *All Manners of Food*, Oxford 1985, pp. 115-6.

[6] See the forthcoming edition of *The Closet of Sir Kenelm Digby Opened* by Peter Davidson and Jane Stevenson (Prospect Books, 1997).

[7] Robert May, *The Accomplisht Cook*, 1660 (facsimile, Totnes, 1994).

An engraving of the portrait of John Evelyn by Sir Godfrey Kneller done for Samuel Pepys, 1689.

Bibliography

This book could not have taken the shape it has without W.G. Hiscock's *John Evelyn and his Family Circle* (London, 1955) nor reference to E.S. de Beer's masterly edition of *The Diary of John Evelyn* in six volumes (Oxford, 1955). The recent version of the diary: Guy de la Bédoyère, *The Diary of John Evelyn* (Bangor, 1994) has been useful as a resource of convenience, and a modern bibliography of Evelyn. The same editor's *The Writings of John Evelyn* (Woodbridge, 1995) is again most convenient, and contains a text of *Sylva*, a work not found in W. Upcott's *The Miscellaneous Writings of John Evelyn, Esq., FRS* (London, 1825). Earlier editions of the diary, depending on the initial work of William Bray, are also of help for the correspondence they reprint. *Diary of John Evelyn*, ed. William Bray, with a life of the author by H.B. Wheatley, published by Bickers, London, 1879, in four volumes, is the edition consulted here. The careful chronology and exact descriptions contained in Geoffrey Keynes, *John Evelyn, A Study in Bibliophily* (Cambridge, 1937) have also proved most useful.

Work on the text of the receipts would have been much more difficult had it not been for the masterly edition of *Martha Washington's Booke of Cookery* by the American historian Karen Hess. Her explanations of points in a manuscript of similar date to Evelyn's threw much light on abstruse meanings and phrases. Similarly, glossaries to and commentaries on seventeenth- and eighteenth-century cookery books and manuscripts that have been published in this century have been of particular assistance: Elizabeth David's to John Nott, Alan Davidson's to Hannah Glasse and Robert May, Hilary Spurling's to Elinor Fettiplace, and Madeleine Masson's to Rebecca Price, all of which are listed below.

Martha Bradley, *The British Housewife* (1756), vol. I, ed. Gilly Lehmann, facsimile ed., Totnes 1996.

Richard Bradley: *The Country Housewife and Lady's Director* (1736), facsimile ed. London 1980, with glossary by Caroline Davidson.

Cambridgeshire Libraries, *Mrs Cromwell's Cookery Book*, Peterborough 1983.

Piero Camporesi, *The Exotic Brew*, trans.Christopher Woodall, Cambridge 1994.

Carter, Charles, *The Complete Practical Cook*, 1730, facsimile, London 1984.

The Compleat Cook and *A Queens Delight* (1655), London 1984.

Elizabeth David, *Harvest of the Cold Months*, London 1994.

Alan Davidson, *Fruit*, London 1991.

Dawson, Thomas, *The Good Housewife's Jewel* (1596–7), eds. Maggie Black & A. Bagnall, Lewes, 1996.

Kenelm Digby, *The Closet of Sir Kenelm Digby Knight Opened*:, ed. Anne Macdonell, London 1910.

Christopher Driver & Michelle Berriedale-Johnson, *Pepys at Table*, London 1984.

John Evelyn, *Acetaria* (1699), Totnes 1996.

Hannah Glasse, *The Art of Cookery Made Plain and Easy* (1747), facsimile ed. under the title *First Catch your Hare, The Art of Cookery Made Plain and Easy*, Totnes 1995.

Geoffrey Grigson, *The Englishman's Flora*, London 1987 ed.

Dorothy Hartley, *Water in England*, London 1964.

Dorothy Hartley, *Food in England*, London 1954 (1975 imp.).

Karen Hess, *Martha Washington's Booke of Cookery*, New York 1981.

Gervase Markham, *The English Hus-wife*, London 1615.

Robert May, *The Accomplisht Cook* (1660), glossary by Alan Davidson, facsimile, Totnes 1994.

John Nott, *Cooks and Confectioners Dictionary* (1726), Elizabeth David ed., facsimile, London 1980.

Jane O'Hara-May, *The Elizabethan Dietary of Health*, Lawrence Kansas, 1977.

Samuel Pepys, *The Diary of Samuel Pepys*, eds. R. Latham & W. Matthews, London 1983.

Hugh Plat, *Delightes for Ladies* (1602), eds. G.E. & K.R. Fussell, London 1948

Rebecca Price, *The Compleat Cook*, Madeleine Masson comp., London 1974.

Hilary Spurling, *Elinor Fettiplace's Receipt Book*, London 1986.

C. Anne Wilson, *Food and Drink in Britain*, London 1973.

List of Receipts

72. To fry a loine of veal.
73. Fricassy a calves head.
74. fry'd hartic.
75. Souc'd pig or turkey.
76. A quaking pudding.
77. Oysters stewed.
78. Loaves Buttered.
– [bis]. A thistle sallade.
79. Puffes.
80. Cheesecakes.
81. A Cake. very light but not rich
    – good
82. Sullibub.
83. Creame Caudell.
84. Creame tarts.
85. Sasages.
86. Barley creame.
87. Curranscakes.
88. Liver pudding.
89. Fine hogs pudding.
90. Oglio spanish.
91. Bisk. French.
92. Spannish Bondejo.
93. Manjar Blanc.
94. Cabbage farced.
95. Turon.
96. To preserve fresh fish.
97. Per far salidi di Bologna.
98. To make a marrow pudding.
99. To make Creame lemon.
100. The manner of making Creame
     at Soteville by Roane.
101. To pickle Cowcumb.
102. To season Cherries (Earle of
     Chesterfield).
l03. To make Mead.
104. To make Raspberry wine.
105. To make Julyflower wine.
106. A Beatillo pie.
107. To marinate flesh.
108. [Receipt omitted.]
109. To make a Black Pudding.
110. To make Puddings of Wine.

111. To make Taffata tarts.
112. To make French Barley
     puddings.
113. To make a winter cheese.
114. To make Angelots.
115. To make a Chesnutt salad.
116. To make chesnutt pies.
117. To make oyster Pyes.
118. To make a cold harsh.
119. To make a harsh of fresh
     Salmon.
120. To make sallads of Lemmons
     and Orenges.
121. To pickel Colliflowers Ginney
     Beanes Samphier or reddish
     Roots.
122. To make a minced Sallade.
123. To boile Tripes.
124. To boile a peece of Beef.
125. To dresse an ele. to stew it.
126. To make red sacke.
127. To make Cracknells.
128. Wotton Alle.
129. Morello or Cherry Wine.
130. Beere.
[131.] Sallad. Ashenkeys
132. To make snow.
133. To make an Almond Custard.
134. To make puffe-past.
135. To make neates tongues red:
136. Sack posset.
137. A good Cake.
138. A Tansy.
139. An Excellent Silibub.
140. To make an Excellent Rich
     Cake.
141. Mince Pies.
142. A Greene Tart.
143. To stew Carps.
144. To make a Plaine Cake.
145. To make a Collar of Beefe.
146. A very good cake. Mrs
     Black[wood?].

211. A new sort of biscuit. L Barckly.
212. To make Waffers.
213. To make Beaue Bread.
214. To make a blanch creame.
215. To make leach.
216. A silibub without a thinne bottom.
217. A fine silibub. Lady Tuke.
218. To picle Broome Buds.
219. To pickle cowcumbers.
220. An other way the lesse greene and are lesse sharp.
221. A Carrot pudding.
[222.] Elder berie wine L[ady] Sheine.
223. To make Birch Wine.
224. Black berrie Wine or Elderberrie Wine. Mr Slingsby.
225. Heath Ale. Lady Mordaunt.
226. To counterfet Renish wine.
227. To make Ice and snow in the Ice.
228. An Apple Puding.
229. A Baked pudding.
230. A Baked oatmell puding.
231. To stew a Rump of beefe.
232. Collops of Beefe.
233. To pickle French beans.
234. To keep Damsons all the yeare[.]
235. Rice pudings in gutts.
236. The Wootton reciet for liver pudings such as they call folks pudings.
237. An Egge Marmalat puding.
238. An Orenge puding.
239. To make a white wine posset[.]
240. To make a slight posset.
241. To make a sack possett with Milk.
242. A Clouted Creame.
243. To make calves foot jelly.
244. To make Naples biscuit.
245. A Goosberie foole with Creame.
246. Goosberie foole without creame.
247. A quaking pudding.
248. To make a puffe puding with suet.
249. Rice pancakes.
250. A foole of any fruit.
251. To make a sallet of smelts. very good.
252. Almond pudings.
253. Neats tongue puddings.
254. To drie Neats toungs.
255. A custard Puding.
256. A Pennyroyall Puding.
257. A Soft Puding or cource White Pott.
258. Elderwine Mrs Bindy.
259. To make french Biscuit upon paper.
260. To make shrewsbery Cakes.
261. To make a sort of Browne waffers.
262. To pickle Cowcumbers like Mango. this is twice.
263. To make a Hartichoke Pie.
264. To dresse a Pike.
265. A good sillybub.
266. Litle puffe pudings.
267. A Fryday or puffe puding. this is twice.
268. To make a light plum cake. Oven glased.
269. To make French Bread.
270. To make Fritters.
271. To make Duch waffers.
272. Fryday puding. [Receipt omitted.]
273. An Almond puding to bake.
274. To make white oatmeall pudings or icings.

To make Angelots.

Take one of your winter Cheeses, when it is a fortnight or three weeks old, and
paer it well, then breake it well with your hands, then putt a prettie deale of
clouted Creame to it, thick and smart, and mixe them well together, then wett
your Cheffat, it must be a deep round one. to take asunder in faire water, then
putt it in and presse it well. and it is made.

115.

To make a Chesnutt sallad.

Take Chesnutts, and boile them till they will Shell, pull off the Huskes, and slice
them thin, then take the Juice of two or tree Lemmons, a Lemmon or two
minced, mingle them with your Chesnutts, and put to them as much hard
sugar as will please your pallat, when you have dish'd it up. put to it a
litle Claret wine.

116.

To make Chesnutt Pies.

Boile them as formerlie for the Sallade, when they are blanched, cutt them in
twinces, put to them whole Sorrell, Lemmons, graps or barberris, a prettie
quantitie of sugar, dates sliced. beaten ginger, And a good proportion of Butter
when they come out of the oven take some uerjuice butter & sugar, beat them well
together and fill up your pie.

A copy of part of the text of the manuscript, written by the clerk
Richard Hoare.

Booke. iiii.
Receipts of Cookery

1.   *Wormewood Ale.*[*]

Brew Ale of a midle strength, put it into a Barrel of 4 Gallons, and
when it hath wroughte what it will, then take a handfull and a halfe
of wormewood whole, of red docks roots whole iiii uncia that be
very young scraped cleane and washed, put the Wormewood and
Dock rootes in a Hippocratic sleeve in a cleane linnen Bag, hang it
in the midle of the Vessell, rolling and stirring it up and downe both
wayes often, then let it repose till it be stale, drinke hereof every
morning at 4 or 5 of the clock, and sleep after it. this is the Lor. M.
of Winchesters[†] receit for the shortness of Breath and is excellent.

[2.]   *Austins Ale.*

Uncia (8 dragms) of Senna uncia Polypod uncia Anniseeds uncia
Fennel and Barberry seeds aña[§] with some sliced Ginger; Bruise all
these together put them in a small linnen bag, and the same into a
vessell of new ale of one gallon, or into a pott for 24 houres. then
drinke of the same in the morning, first fasting, and last at going to
Bed – blood warme, this will cleanse the Bodie, and procure a good
stomach; you may use the same every moneth in the yeare, if you
find your selfe disposed.

---

[*] This first section, until Receipt 127, was written by Evelyn's clerk and amanuensis, Richard Hoare. The titles were written in the right-hand margin, and the
receipts themselves in a fine, shapely italic hand.

[†] Presumably John Paulet, fifth marquis (1598–1675), royalist, defender of Basing
House, Hampshire.

[§] i.e. of each the same.

3.   Scurvy Grasse beere.

Scurvy grasse, wash it, and spread it on a table for 24 houres, that it dry well, let there be of it one pecke lb vi,[‡] also water cresses, Brook lyme and Betony of each 4 handfulls, and of sage three handfulls, bruise and stampe all these in a mortar, saxafras uncia ii sliced into small chippes, nutmeg uncia i, mace, cloves of each a quar: of an ounce, as you think good; these spices to be beaten grosse, then put them into [a] Hippocratic sleeve, (or a Bolster Bag) and so hang them in a firkin of beere, of eight oz to shill: the barrell and in quantity eight or 10 Gallons.

4.   Wormewoode Beere.

Gather wormewoode in May and lay it upon a sheete, and turn it over, a day or two, till it be drye, then gather dock roote between michaelmas and Alhalowtide, wash them very cleane, and pick out the rotten, then dry them as the wormewood, then take a firkin of iii Gall. and fill it with ordinary beere then put in of dry Wormewoode iii uncia and of dock rootes uncia i, sliced, put it in when the beere hath almost done working, and store it a good while till most of it sinke to the Bottome, after 3 weekes drinke of it.

5.   An Almond Florendine.[*]

R.[†] Marrow, halfe as much grated Bread, 3 or 4 yolkes of egges, boiled hard, and minced small, a few currans, a few pickeled Barberyes, 3 or 4 slices of Lemmons, cut into litle pieces, 6 dates cut into quarters, a good hanfull of blanched Almonds beaten small, and in their beating adde to them a qtr. of a pinte of Creame, 2 or three spoonefulles of Rosewater; mingle all these together seasoned with

---

‡ This seems a double note of quantity, 1 peck (by volume) or 6 lbs (by weight).
* Compare the recipe of the same name in John Nott's *Cooks Dictionary* (1726).
† i.e. *R[ecipe]* or Take (from the Latin: imperative of the verb *recipere*, to receive).

a little salt, sugar, Cinnamon, and nutmeg, then lay this in a Puffe paste, and let it bake about an houre and an halfe.

6. Puffes.

R. new milke cheese curds, straine them mingle them with a little fine floure, and new milke, 7 egges yolkes, mix all together these ingredients, and make it like batter, then take a pye plate, and butter it a litle, drop then the batter in reasonable great Lumpes, and bake them in a softly heated oven, the sauce may be sugar, Cinnamon, butter and vineger, so strewing sugar on them, serve them up.

7. Pease Pottage.

Boile pease three or 4 houres, with a litle salt, pepper and ginger, about halfe an houre ere you take it off, adde a sprig of tyme, store of Minte, then when thoroughly boiled take it off, straine it in setting it over a Chafing dish, put to it some few leaves of Sorrell, a peice of fresh butter, Parmizan Cheese scraped on the top, if you have it, this is most rare.

8. French Broath.

Take mutton or Pidgeons boile them, then when be scummed, put in as much French Barley, as will thicken the Broath; first boiling the Barley in three severall waters, till it Cracks, then put in Raisins of the sunne, a litle mace, with a litle pickeld parseley, when tis boiled adde a litle sweet butter to the Broath. the Sippetts now in use wherewith this must be served for white Broaths are made of Puffe past, cut in fashion of Lozenges, baked and put in a dish.

9. Pease pottage.

Take nine quarts of water, poure it into a Brasse pott, put into it a quart and a halfe of good peas (if not very excellent, two quarts) 2 pound of rib bacon, boile them together till the peas be well boiled, then take out the peas, & put them into a Cullender, and mash them with a Ladle, and as you mash them, powre into them the quantity of three quarts of water, till you have washed all the goodnesse out of them, then take that which runnes through the Cullender, and returne it into the Pott again, then take an handfull of dryed mint, 20 pepper Cornes, and of Coriander seeds one ounce, being all pounded small, put it into the pot letting it boile an houre, in the meane while set on a porrenger with a pound of butter, 3 cloves of Garlicke, one handfull of parseley and a small onyon, all of which being minced very small, put into the butter, and let it boile a quarter of an hour, then cut bread in thin slices, spread them with butter and lay themm in the dish, then put into the dish also two spoonefulls of white wine vineger, and lastly fill the dish with the Pease pottage: this is the French olio, and excellent dish.

10.   *Almond butter.* Very good.[†]

Breake 4 new egges, and beat them with a pinte of good creame, then straine them from the Cocke treadings & boil them on an easy fire, stirring them continually till they be well curded, then put them into a Cloath, that their whay may passe from the Curd, put thereto the like weight of blanched almonds beaten very fine with sugar and rose water, then beaten together all in a morter, lastly sweeten it with sugar, the more egges, the more yellow it will be.

11.   *Banbury Cake.*

Take a pinte ['peck' *is added above the line*] of fine flowre, half an ounce of nutmeg, as much of Cinnamon beaten and searsed, [pound and a half][¶] of butter, 10 egges, put out 4 of the whites, a pinte and a qtr. of good ale Yeast, beat your egges very well, straine them and

---

† Added comment.
¶ Supplied.

your yeast with a Litle warme water, then put in the butter cold in litle Bitts (the water wherewith you knead must be scalding hott) thus make it good paste, then lay it to rise in a warme cloath a qur of an houre; then put in a pound of raisins stoned and cut in sunder and a pound of Currants, half a pound of powdered sugar finely beaten, and mingled with the Currants, a litle muske and Ambergrece dissolved in 4 good spoonefulls of rose water, the currans must be made exceeding drye, else they will make the cake heavy, breake the paste in litle peices into the kneading pan or trough, and lay and lay* of past, and then a lay or bed of Currans, till all be spent, mingle the past, and Currans very well, but take heed of breaking the Currans, then make it up and cutt it one inch in the sides or edge,† and so let it stand in oven two hours – beate a litle rosewater and searsed sugar, with a litle white of egges till they looke very white, with this – wash your Cake all over the top with a feather, and set all in the oven till it be drye, the oven being heated as for manchetts.

12.   the lady Harringtons§ cake.

Take a pecke of fine flowre, season it as you please with Cinnamon, Nutmegs, cloves and mace all beaten small and one spoonefull of Carraway seeds, some salt q. s.,# about a pinte of Ale yeast, then make a posset with two quarts of good Creame when it boiles up, put to it a pinte of sack, sweeten it also with some Sugar, and (being so

---

* Presumably the copyist intended 'and lay a lay', i.e. lay a layer.

† The instruction to cut the cake around the perimeter was to enable it to rise in the oven, as one would slash a loaf of bread. For notes on making such great cakes, see Hess. Gervase Markham has a recipe for Banbury cake, and *The Compleat Cook* gives a recipe from the Countess of Rutland, 'so much praised at her Daughter's Wedding.'

§ This may be a reference to the family of the Barons Harington of Exton in Rutland, or to Catherine, wife of Sir James Harrington, parliamentarian, cousin of the republican author of *Oceana*, and occupant of the mansion at Swakeley, Ickenham until 1665, see Pepys's diary.

i.e. q[uantum] s[ufficit], as much as is sufficient.

coole as it scald not the yeast) with this posset knead your flowre thus made into paste cover it with a warme cloath, and so let it lye a while by the fire to rise, then have ready eight pounds of Currans cleane picked and well rubbed drye with a cloath, worke all your Currance by a few at once into your paste, leaving onely a peice of your past without fruit to cover the Toppe, and bottome of the Cake which must be rowled out thin and worked and so laied on, as it meet about the sides of the cake, when you have so closed it that it is as big as you desire it; then cut it round with a knife as you doe man-chett, then prinke and pricke it, & bake* it in the oven heated up as for manchetts, if it browne oremuch spread a Paper on it; a Cake of a peck may stand in the oven two houres; if lesse, lesse time will serve.

13. Cakes of Currance.

Take your Currance put them in a litle pott with rose water and set it in a skellet of boiling water to plumpe, then make your Paste Lithe; that it may rowle very thin then take what spices you like best finely beaten; if you please you may colour your past with saffron water, rowle a sheet of past upon which lay some Currance in a small round Compasse, then lay another sheet of paste on the Currance and rowle them pretty thin so that the Currans may appeare through, then cut them round with an iron, and prick them very well.

14. Pancakes.

R. of Rice lb ∫∫† and boile it very tender, [*interlineated note:* in 3 pints of water] then bruise it very small, then take 8 egges [*interlineal:* or 9 leave out (3 crossed out) 4 whites] boile halfe a pinte of Creame, and adde to your rice and [*an illegible word, but*

---

* 'Bake' is interlineally inserted over a deleted 'heat'.
† The ∫∫ is a sign used by the scribe R. Hoare to indicate a half [pound].

overwritten with: 6 ounces of butter melted flower one spoonfull] and salt with a litle nutmeg and Sugar, mingle all these together and fry them with butter in a pan. if they are made over night it is best.[†]

15. Cheese.

An excellent Cheeze cheshire, Cheddar Parmizan being cut into 4 quarters or whole, and put into good sallet oyle, renders it most excellent, it may be kept so a yeare 2 or 3 if you please nor is the oyle one jott the worse.

16. An Almond Custard.

Take a quart. of Creame, boile it with a litle Large mace, (when boyled, take some Isinglasse, and steep it an houre or two in rosewater,) then with the rose water put it into the Creame, boile it till the Isinglasse be consumed, then take a quarterne[*] of sweet Jordan Almonds, blanched and beaten well, put them into the Creame letting it boile very well with 3 or 4 yolkes of egges, then take it from the fire season it with sugar, straine all in a Dish, when cold eat it.

17. Barley Cream.

Take an handfull of french Barley, boile it in a sufficient quantity of running water till the Barley be tender, then straine the Barley from the water, stampe it in a stone morter with a few blanched Almonds, and so grind them together with some of the water wherein the barley was boiled, then strain it, and put to it a quantity of red rose water, and sugar, then boile it a litle againe with a few large mace and Cinnamon.

---

† Added note. Compare this receipt to the more finished version at no 249, below.
* The receipt does not state a quarter of what; presumably a quarter of a pound.

18. *Mangar blanch.*

R. a quart of fresh milke, put into it a pound of the finest floure of Rice, the Brawne of an Hen newly killed, and so boiled that the brawne may be pulled in little small thredds like haires, put this into the Milke [*before the word* 'Milke', 'Bed' *has been deleted*], boile them together, perpetually stirring them together, at the end put in a pound of sugar, still stirring it, and adding a litle rosewater; put it then on a plate and it will come off cleane from the plate if sufficiently boiled; for this is the tryall, then put it into a dish, and serve it like marmalade in slices. It will keep 4 or 6 dayes and is excellent to carry on a long journey.

19. *To dresse a Rabbet.*

Set a Rabbet well in a pott, with the Liver, then take him out and cut him in 4 or 5 peices, then put him in a faire dish with a good handfull of Parseley minced small with a litle bundle of time and three or 4 Apples quartered, some sugar, 4 blades of large mace halfe a pinte of clarret wine, one handfull of Currants, one or two ounces of butter; then fill it up with water and set it astewing together, until it be tender, keeping it very close-covered, then put in an whole onyon, and so serve it upon sippetts with a garnish.

20. *Pig brawne.*

Take a great fat pig, scald him, take out all the Bones, rowle the sides as you doe brawne, but in the rowling put here and there litle peices a whole mace and sliced pepper,[†] tye the collars with basse or tape, then boile them in water and salt, then souce them; let the souceing drinke be made of water vinegar and salt; when you serve it you must cut the collar in three parts and put them in one dish, the sauce is vinegar.

---

† It is likely that the copyist should have written 'sliced ginger' not 'pepper'.

21.   To dresse a leg of venson.

Take a leg from the hanch (when the meat is cutt off for a Pasty) and powder it 4 dayes or a weeke, then stuffe it with parseley and boile it; serve it thus at the second course being cold with mustard & sugar.

22.   Venison that shall keep an yeere.

Take the Bones out of the venison, and season it with pepper and salt, thus let it lye seasoned one whole night before you bake it, and roule it, and put it in a pot as you thinke fitt, cover the pott when you bake it, then let it stand at least six houres in the oven to make it tender, and when you draw it forth put the Liquor very cleane out of the pott and fill it up with very good butter (which you must have ready,) whilst is yet hot but first you must well clarifie the butter and be sure that the venison be covered with Butter when it is cold. You must close up the pott with paper and Bladders, that it receive no aire at all, else all is lost.*

23.   To boile a Carpe (or Pike).

Take a faire melt Carpe and scoure him well with salt, then wash him very cleane and dry him well with a Cloath, then lay him in a faire dish and put under him three or 4 spoonesfulls of white wine vinegar and cut off the head first, and let him bleed well and then open him well and take out the gutts and Livour (but take heed of breakeing the Gall) then take off the fatt from the gutts and cut of the taile a good length and cleane the midle peice so let it lye in the dish bleeding untill your liquour be boiling. Now to boile him, take as much clarret wine as you thinke will cover him in a skellet, and put in some large mace, sliced nutmeg, and sliced ginger, a litle bundle of Rosemary and tyme, two whole Onyons and when it boiles then

---

* The last sentence is an additional note in another hand.

put in the white wine vinegar, with the bloud which is in the dish, and so put in the Carpe, letting it boile a good pretty while, but a litle before you take him up, put in a peice of butter as big as a walnutt and serve him up with sliced lemon and Barberies, sippets &c. the liquor which is left will serve to boile another, after the same manner you may boile a Pike, omitting only the blood.

24. Goose.

The Italians put a clove of Garlic in the Bodie of most fowle, but in my mind it doth in nothing better, then in a goose or turkey, in which last wee also use to stick Cloves.[†]

25. choosing of fowle.

To choose foule, those which are old have the mouth yellow and greenish within, eyes sunke low, and a greenish colour at the tailes. Hens with eggs though dead are read at the Ghills, else they be pale.

26. [Fowl]

Fowle must be tied to the spit (by no meanes thrust through with a spitt or wooden Pricks) with some butter in their Bodies; tye necks and rumpe so as no Ayre gets in.

27. Fowle.

Fowle must be basted with fresh butter, being cold on the spitt, not before tis roasted, or the butter melted in the Pan &c.

28. Wallnuts.

Walnuts peeled put into clarret wine and salt, some use salt & water.

---

† Sir Kenelm Digby would agree with Evelyn ('You may boil Garlick in the belly of the fouls, if you like it'), but Robert May, and John Nott after him, confine themselves to the more traditional spices of nutmeg, mace, cloves and bay.

29. *To dresse a Capon after the Italian.*

Cut a Capon in very thin small slices, put to him some pickeld broome Buddes, 4 or 5 minced hard yolkes of egges, a Litle minced lemmon, without the kernells, a litle of Clarret wine, some sweet butter, so serve him up with Sippetts with the rump & wings.

30. *Monkes watergrewell.*

R. A marrow Bone, and when the marrow is out, cutt him all in Pieces, letting it boile well, then straine it, and put oatmeale greatts therein, and stoned raisins, and mace, a bundle of sweet herbes, and when all is well boiled, beat three or foure yolkes of egges, and some milke to make it white, some sugar, and a spoonefull of rose water.

31. *Skerrit milke.*

Take skerrits, boile them tender, straine them well, let the milke and creame boile with Large mace, and so put in the skerrits, to which (being a litle boiled), put in 3 or 4 yolkes of Egges, and so with sugar it is done.*

32. *Froath or whipt Creams.*

Take a pinte of white wine, and put to it the Juice of two Lemmons, make it very sweet of the finest sugar, then put to it a quart of Creame, stirring it in, then immediatly you must take a whiske, made of dry birchin twigges, and beat it as you doe egges, and as the froth riseth take it off with a spoone, and lay it like sudds in a silver dish or the like, you must tye a bunch of Rosemary, and one of the Lemmon peeles in the whisk, before you beat it.

33. *Meath.*

Take a gallon of water, a quart of honey, and put to it cowslips, Lemmon peele, and boile it for almost an houre, then let it stand till

---

* Compare this recipe to that in *Acetaria*.

it be very cold, and put it up into a Rundlet, and one Lemmon with it: let it so stand two or 3 dayes; then stop it up very close till you drinke it.

34.   To pickle Asparagus.

Take Asparragus, and breake off the hard ends, and put them up into white wine vineger, and salt, according to discretion; so that they be very well covered with vineger, and, when they have this layen six weekes in Pickle, take them quite out, and boile the Pickle or Liquor, and skimme it very well; and if there be need renew it with vineger and salt, and when tis cold put them in againe, and then will it certainely keep an whole yeare, spend these when you please, boiling them till they be enough.*

35.   A spanish foole.

Take 8 or 10 whites of Egges, beat them well, and some Creame, q.s. beat all well together, a litle nutmeg, mace, sugar, and rosewater, and so streyne it, then bake it in a Dish, or Paste, lyke a Pie, as you please, then strew some Carrawayes upon it, but have a care the oven be not too hott, for then it will become all whay.

36.   A florendine Puffe paste.

Take Calves feet, seeth them tender, let them be cold then slice them thin in litle bitts, but they must be seasoned with nutmegs, Cinnamon, sugar, marrow, dates and the yolkes of egges, whitewine beaten together, and two graines of muske steeped in Rosewater, then bake it in Puffe past, and eate it hott.

37.   Lobster pie.

Take a Lobster shred him very small, then season it with Cinnamon, sugar, nutmegs, and a spoonefull of vineger, ambergrece, rosewater,

---

* The recipe for pickled asparagus in *Acetaria* shows certain variations.

muske and butter, thus make it as you doe an Artichoke pie or Potatoe; but bake it not so much, you may rub the bottome of the dish with dry muske, which will make it taste very pleasantly. this is for the second service.

38.   Spinnage pudding

R. a quantity of spinnage, beate it, streyne it well, put to it some grated bread, and eight yolkes of egges, some marrow cut small some Cinnamon and sugar, rosewater, and a few Carrawayes if you can get them, then a litle creame boiled before (for 'twill aske litle baking), and so bake it in a dish with a garnish of Puffe.

39.   Calves foot pudding.

Take 2 Calves feet, shred them very fine, grate a penny Loafe and 2¶ biscuits and halfe a pound of beefe suet,$^\#$ halfe a pound of currance, a litle cloves, mace, and nutmegs beaten a litle rosewater, salt and sugar, 5 egges, worke all these together with your hands, take the sale‡ of a breast of veale, laye it in a litle warme water that it doe not cracke, then you put your pudding in and draw it in together, with thridd through the side which must be pulled out when it is boiled, note that you must wrap it in a cloath when you boile it; the sawce to it is butter, sacke and sugar.

40.   Lady Brownes* Pudding or the Chathern¶ Pudding.

Take halfe a Chalderon the fairest and whitest, and parboile it, then let it coole, and shred it exceeding small, then take an English pinte

---

¶ This figure is a correction, replacing an illegible word.

\# 'Halfe a pound of beefe suet' is written twice, the second time crossed out.

‡ What is meant here is caul. It is unclear whether it is a mistranscription or a word otherwise unrecorded.

* Presumably Lady Elizabeth Browne, née Prettyman (c.1610–52), Mary Evelyn's mother, wife of Sir Richard Browne.

¶ Variant form, now obsolete, of chawdron or chalderon, i.e. entrails.

of sweet creame, 6 eggs two of them without whites; then beat cloves, ginger, Cinamo[n], nutmeg and mace q.s. with a spoonefull rosewater sweetened with sugar, as all the rest sweetned to your liking then shred an handfull of sweet herbs viz parseley, time, marjoram, beetes, and sorrell a litle penny royall with a few Lemons one or two small greene skallions, use a penny Loafe of grated bread, halfe a pound of beefe suet shred; mix all these ingredients together with a quarter of a pound of raisins of the sunne, 3 quarters of currance, a few shred dates, and you may grate in two or three maqueroons or Naples biscuits without seeds and one spoonefull of fine flowre to bind it, also half a pound of marrow in big Lumpes rowled up in the yolke of an egge, put all this into a Bag to boile or in a puffe paste to bake, forget not salt before you put it into the bag. The sauce is sugar, sacke, butter and (as you please) rosewater.

41.   Liver puddings.

Take hogges liver, parboile it, grate it and take as much grated Bread as liver, sweeten with sugar & spice all sorts, (except pepper) to your liking, sweet Creame, and egges, more yolkes than whites, reasonably full of Currance, a spoonefull or two of sack, beefe suett and marrow, maqueroons and biscuits as in the former, a litle musk, mix these together and so fill it in the Gutts.[†]

42.   Bloodings.

Take whole groatts of Oatmeale [or halfe groats rather][*], well pick'd and bruised a litle, then take your blood hott from the hogge, and put in your oatmeale, being well stirred before from the Cloddes, and put in a handfull of salt, thus let it steep two nightes and a day, season it with these hearbs, marjoram a litle handfull, more of tyme,

---

† The reiteration of the note about macaroons and Naples biscuit may indicate that this receipt, too, came from the Browne/Prettyman household.

* Words in square brackets added above the line.

as much as of both of winter savory, as much as all three of Penny royall, sage, parseley, beetes, sorrel, fennell and Cammomile, an handfull of each; two or three greene Leekes, a spoonefull of bruised Fennell seeds, cloves, mace, nutmeg, ginger and a litle pepper and salt, these you must put in shred if greene & rubbed if drye, when you goe to make them; also a quart of milke, scalding hott, 4 or 5 egges, which is sufficient for 4 dozen of puddings, hogs suet as you please, and a litle greated bread[.] some use beefe suet.[*]

43.   Almond pudding.

Take of almonds lb j[‡] blanch them in cold water, beat them with rosewater finely and sugar, then take 8 egges and but 4 of the whites, beat them with rose water, put to them a porrenger full of Cream scalded and halfe penny loafe of grated white bread, a pound of sugar or more as you see cause cinnamon, cloves mace, as you please, two pound of marrow, or beefsuet sliced very small[.] a little Am. greec.[*]

44.   Rice puddings.

Take of Rice lb j[‡] picked cleane, steep it all night in fayre water or new milke, draine out the liquour from it in Cullender as dry as may be, then boile it in some six wine quarts of new milke, till it be very tender and thick; then straine it againe, if it be any thing thinne, put in to 24 yolkes of Egges, and one or two whites, stirring all well together, then put in salt and sugar qua: s: then put to it 3 or 4 grated nutmegs and as much beaten mace, gr. vi[†] Ambergrece, or muske still stirring it, then take 3 pound of oxes marrow shred it, but not over small, then fill the gutts but not too full, then boile the Puddings, but without pricking least the marrow get out, and when cold boile them a second tyme.

---

* Subsequent annotation.   ‡ 'lb j', i.e. 1 lb.
† 'gr vi', i.e. six grains.

45. *Parsenips after the spanish.*

Take the Parsenips, boile them very tender and bruise them all to a Pomate, then take a litle Creame and adde to them, and so make them hott againe, then take some sweet butter to them, and a litle sugar and boile a few Currance, and strew on them, then squeeze the Juice of a Lemmon on them and so serve them with sippetts.[†]

46. *To roast a turkey.*

When the Turkey is on the Spitt and warme, baste him with the sweetest Lard, which being wrapped in a cleane white paper, very hard and stuck on a long forke set on fyre, droppeth in Flames on the fowle; which rendereth the flesh thereof exceedingly plump and tender.

47. *A sallet of Artich.*

Artichokes raw and very young being cutt, and placed like sippetts in a dish eaten with pepper and sugar or salt, or with pepper and oyle, is an excellent rellisher before wine, and is served in Collation[‡] by the french.

48. *A Sellery sallet.*[*]

That which the Italians call selery is smalledge stalkes layed in the earth watered and whited, it is eaten with pepper and oyle or pepper and salt; it is an admirable Sallet, and it is most frequently used in Italy, yet sometymes there is in it a small red worme, which is poison as some say, but holding the stalke 'twixt the Light and your selfe it is easily perceived.

---

† This receipt is in *Acetaria*, though not ascribed to Spain.

‡ The Roman Catholic collation was a last meal, in place of supper, in times of fasting. By extension, it described a snack, a supplementary meal. See this receipt in *Acetaria*, where Dr Muffet is cited as authority, rather than the French.

* This Receipt or comment is the ancestor of the entry in the catalogue of *Acetaria*. Echoes of Receipts 49–52 are also found. For smalledge, see glossary.

49. Fennell sallet.

Fennell stalkes where they knitt and grow pithy are eaten in like maner as a sallet.

50. Orrenge leaves.

Set or sow the seedes of Orenges and Lemmons, and when they first appeare Croppe them and put foure or 5 into any sallet, they render an admirable taste.

51. Sampier.‡

Also the Leaves of raw Sampier, for the seeds will grow without any difficulty.

52. Turnup stalkes.

Let Turneps grow to seedes, then take the stalkes as farre as they will well breake downewards, peele them, bind them in Bunches, and then boile them as you doe esperges: a rare sallet, and Charles the first delight of English sallets.†

53. Sauce robert.

Mustard, vinegar, verjuice, pepper, and onyone, the onyone sliced and put into a skellet, where there is butter or the fatt of the foule for which you make it, in this boile the Onyons to a pappe, and then mix them with the above mentioned ingredients with salt, last of all heat them together over a Chafing dish till they boile; this is the Passe par tout in France, for Turkey, goose, pig, ducks, petitoes* &c:

---

‡ Samphire.
† What he is intending to say is that it was Charles I's favourite salad.
* Pigs' trotters.

54. *For fowle:*[*]

Pull [or cut,] fowle [as woodcocks, snipes, plovers &c:] in peices so soone as they come hott from spitt, then dip them in claret[¶] or other strong wine, and bestow on them good store of Juice of Orrenge, pepper toasts, the chipping of Bread made into small Crumbes salt, set the foule over a Chafing dish, and boile all to a resonable consistence, some adde the peele of orange the yolke of an egge; and then with very litle nutmeg it serves for Capon sauce.

55. *Tripes.*

Tripes broyled on the Gridiron are to be eaten with pepper and vineger, with a litle salt, having been first well boiled.

56. *Sauce douce.*

Pepper, vineger, sugar, Cinamon, boile this to a thicknesse, and it is rare for the hare, and Duck.

57. *Mustard.*

R. the best mustard seedes, and put them into faire water: fling a way all that swiming on the top, for it is empty and worth nothing, wash it thus three or 4 times, then rub it exceedingly drye, with warme linnen cloaths then powder it in a morter, and searse it in a fine Cue;[§] then temper it with the Juice of horse reddish rootes and put some Sugar in it to sweeten it, then put it into a Gally pott, corke it very close, and put a bladder over it, and after a moneth you have the most exquisite mustard that can be eaten: Take of the same mustard, put to it gravy, verjuice, sugar, clarret wine & Lemmon, and you may make an Admirable sauce for any foule or fish.

---

[*] This receipt is much annotated in another hand. The amendments or qualifications are here printed within the square brackets.
[¶] 'Claret' is substituted for 'sacke' which has been crossed out.
[§] For 'cue', see glossary.

58. *Venison and Turkey sauce.*

Take a Manchet, pare off the Crustes, slice it into thin slices put thereto claret wine, a litle whole cinamon, 2 or three cloves a litle sliced nutmeg, with sugar to sweeten it, let this boile a good while, breake the bread no more, then when you turne it, if you desire it red, R.[†] red sanders and putt it into a cloath rubbing it into clarret wine, and let it boile together, if it be a Gallendine for a turkey, you must straine the bread with the Clarret wine and leave out the spice: so it serves for venison and Turkey.

59. *To stewe a neck of mutton with Cowcumbers.*

Take a large necke of mutton, joynt it well, spitt it bake roste it, then draw it off and cutt every bone in sunder but save the gravy in a stewing pan with the mutton, then take a cowcumber or two, pare off all the white, then cut it in Large slices pretty thick and cutt it across againe that they may be like dice; then put it into a Dish with salt and a litle sliced pepper, so let it stand still[‡] store of Liquour cometh from it, then put it into the stewing pan to the mutton, and let it stew till it be tender, then dish it on sippetts and put to the liquor a good peice of sweet butter, then lastly poure all the Liquor on the meate.

60. *Snow houses.*[¶]

To coole drinkes the Invention of conserving: snow is very usefull which is this: first digge a pitte on the side of some shady hill or

---

† '*R[ecipe]*' = take.
‡ *Recte* 'till'.
¶ This paragraph relating to ice houses prefigures Evelyn's communication of details concerning Italian ice houses to the scientist and fellow-member of the Royal Society, Robert Boyle, which he published in *New Experiments & Observations Touching Cold* in 1683. He not only quoted Evelyn, but included a graphic illustration of the pit that Evelyn describes here. For more information on ice houses, see Elizabeth David, *Harvest of the Cold Months*, and Monica Ellis, *Ice and Icehouses through the Ages*.

rising, because of the descent of the water, line the pit with reeds, Bulrushes or straw, but bulrushes or Sedge being the best. About a foot from the Bottome of the Pitt must be erect[ed] a strong frame on which must be layed a grate [of] strong round wood, upon this lay a bed of straw, upon the straw a Bed of the cleanest snow, and this so beaten down with rammers till it become as it were a stone or Ice; after this lay thereon as much straw as before, viz. about halfe a foot in thicknesse upon this snow beaten as before, continuing this order of snow and straw, stratum super stratum, till the pitt be full, provided that the superficies be well covered with straw, over all this is a pyramidall frame to be erected about 12 foot high according to discretion which being thatched very thick will preserve the aire, and hott sunne from penetrating, and so conserve the snow for many yeares, although something will melt sinke and be lost, for which end that grate and distance from the grate to the ground is left, when you will use thereof cut it with an Instrument into wedges like butter and put it into Contemplores or Glasses, made for the Purpose in these formes. se:[*] Tit: Med: Num: 25/3.[‡]

A  B

* An abbreviation of 'See'.
‡ This bibliographic reference has not been located.

A Contemplore¶ made of Corke as bigg as a Gallon and like in shape, onely the materials are corke and hath a moveable cover, through which there is an hole in the midle, all joinctures being well closed with Pitch. In this vessel you put in your snowe made small about the glass bottle whose necke appeares through the cover as in fig. A.

The other Is made entirely of glasse and needs no other description.

61.   Lemmonade.

R. wine one part, water 3, in which slice a juicy Lemmon, hanging the rind about the glasse, sweeten it well with the best sugar, and one drop of spirit of vitriol, with one Amber comfitt.

62.   [Orange drink.]*

Orenge juice, sugar and fontaine water well brewed together, is an excellent drinke to coole, may be used both in feavours and hot salt Rhumes.

63.   [Water to drink.]*

Water alone brewed too and fro with good crummes of bread maketh a very good drinke if the Pott be let stand that the Crummes may

---

¶ Much has been written about contemplores or *cantimplora* (of Spanish origin) by the late Elizabeth David, both in correspondence with the present editor (see the glossary, below), and in her book, cited above. She underlines, as does Evelyn with these illustrations, the distinction between two forms of cantimplora: the first (A) was essentially an ice bucket into which a bottle was thrust to be chilled by surrounding snow; the second (B) was a carafe with a long and distinctive spout. The wine in the carafe was cooled by a container packed with snow that was introduced through the top. The French had long-spouted watering cans called *chantepleures* which looked like the carafe here illustrated. More about cantimplora in seventeenth-century Tuscany may be found in Piero Camporesi, *Exotic Brew*. The drawings reproduced here have been copied from the original MS by the editor.

* Title supplied, omitted in the MS.

settle and this is of excellent use with Travellours, when good beere
is not to be had.

64. [Mushrooms.]*

Take Mushrooms that are white above and red underneath, such as
grow in Gardens, medowes, hilles, and on Dunghills raised for the
Purpose, by no means such as grow in the woodes, or on old
stumpes, and shady places, wash them very well then boile them
halfe a quarter of an houre or more, then drye them very well in a
Napkin, pressing the water utterly out from them: whilst they are yet
hott, putt melted Butter amongst them with an Onyon, then season
them with Pepper and salt, and thus you may fry them, or stew them,
with a litle vineger or white wine. If you must take off the Skin and
pare away the bottoms of them Se: Receipt: 95.¶

65. Almond milke.

Take a good bigg Chicken and stoppe it full of Buglasse & Parsley,
then sett it a boiling in three pints of water till it be tender, you must
put in the boiling two or three flakes of mace with a Bundle of
Buglosse, and a sprig of Rosemary & thyme, and when it is boiled
set it a cooling then take a quarter of a pound of Almonds, blanch
them and beat them in a stone morter very fine, and as you beat them
you add now and then a spoonefull of the Chicken broth to keep
them from oiling, and when they be very fine put the Chicken broth
into the morter to the Almonds, grinde them well together straine it
into a possett pott and put as much sugar as will make it sweet, cutt
a Nutmeg in fower, and put into it a litle whole Cinnamon, 2 graines
of muske, 3 graines of Ambergreece, 6 spoonefulls of Rosewater, let

---

* Title supplied, omitted in the MS.

¶ Se:: i.e. see. This cross reference is mistaken, the extra receipt for mushrooms
may be found at 91, where it forms the second half of the receipt.

all these boile together half an houre; and then take it off, and put it into a glass, and keep it for your use.

66. *Strong jelly.*

Take veale or Calves feet, and boile it to the quantity of a quart, then straine it, and let it stand till it be cold, then pour it into a skillet, with half a Pinte of White wine, and a litle sacke if you please; and a pound and halfe of Sugar to sweeten a quart, and of Cinnamon nutmegs & Ginger as much as you thinke fitt to have it taste strong of the Spices, when all these are put together in the skillet, beat too whites of egges together till they come to froth, and put them to the Jelly in the Skillet, and let all boile together a small tyme, till it be clarified, then let it run through a Jelly bag, if you please, you may putt in a spoonefull or two of Rosewater when it comes.

67. *Jelly of veale.*

Take a shoulder or a good knuckle of veale and cutt off all the fatt of i[t]*, then lay it a soaking in faire conduit water one night, then take it, and wash it in warme water, and take out all the bleeding vaines, then take one gallon of faire conduit water, and put your veale into it, and sett it upon the fire in a new or very cleane pipkin, and boile it up a good pac[e]* with a cleare fire and skimme all the fatt of it very cleane, and when it is allmost boiled half away then take up a spoonefull and put it in some cold dish, and when you see it will Jelly stiffe; then take it off the fire and straine it through a cloath into an earthen dish; and when it is cold take all the fatt off it, then you must take the white of an egge; and a quarter of a pinte of Rosewater, beat it up to a froath then put it into a skillet that will hold two quarts then take out [a]* quart of your Jelly and put to it, then put to it half a pound of double refined sugar or more if you will

---

* Supplied.

have it sweet, then put in the Juice of 4 or 5 Lemmonds, then take
a quarter of a pinte of the sharpest white wine you can gett, and putt
it into the Jelly, if you cannot have lemmons put in a spoonefull of
the best white wine vineger, then take 2 races of Ginger, and pare off
the rind and slice it thin, then take one sticke of Cinnamon, or a
spoonefull of the best Cinnamon Water; then take 2 or 3 toppes of
the sprigs of Rosemary; half a spoonfull of Coliander seeds rubbed
cleane put all them into the Jelley; and set it upon a cleare charcoale
fire, and keep [it]‡ stirring it softly with a spoone, untill [it boile]‡
it boile up, when it is turned like a possett and the Jelley looks cleane
under the skumme, take it off the fire, then put the rinde of a Lemon
and a sprigge or two of Rosemary into the bottom of the Jelley
bagge, then take the Jelley and runne it through the Jelley bagge two
or three tymes into some potts or glasses for your use.

68. *To Bake venison or beefe to keep all the yeare.*

Take a haunch of venison, and cut off the postle, it being the sinewy
part of the leg, leaving a large fillet as you doe of veale, taking the
bone out of the flesh as whole as you can, then take pepper salt mace
nutmeggs cloves, the least of your spices being the sweet spices, and
the least of all cloaves, mix your seasoning alltogether, stopping
your venaison therewith as you would beefe with parsely, then rolle
it up close together, and put the fattside of your venison downewards
into the Pott, covering it all over [with]* 2 lb of fresh butter, then
cover it with a Platter, and stoppe it close with your paste, then put
it into the oven it being as hott as for venison, letting it stand in the
oven an hower longer than you would a pasty of venison. Then draw
it out and open the pots and lay a trencher on the toppe of the meat
as it swimmeth sinking it downe with a weight, till the butter cover

‡ These words are superfluously repeated in the MS.
* Supplied.

66

the trencher, so let it stand till it be cold then lay on your platter again and keep it so.

69.   Neats tongue pies.

Take 2 neats tongues and halfe boile them and when they be cold pare and mince them very small, then mince 4 [lb]* Beefe suett very small by itselfe; and put in therewith 2 ounces of nutmegs, 1 pound of Currans, [the same]* of raisins of the sunne, and a litle Sugar, a litle rosewater and verdjuice, and an apple or two minced very small. put in a few Anniseeds and a litle orrange peele, and if you will salt.

70.   Neats tongue pies.

Take the neats tongue being roasted and pared, and cutt into thin slices, and steep it all night in verdjuice and season with it a litle nutmeg cloves and mace and Cinnamon. Then lay it in the pye with a great deale of Butter and when it is almost enough take it out of the oven and cutt it, if you have made no vent, and put in some claret wine and Sugar so much as you shall thinke fit, then sett it into the oven againe and let it stand till it be enough, then serve it up with a litle Scraped Sugar.

71.   A chine of Beefe baked.

Take a Chine of beefe, the lesser end of it unsalted, and beat it very well with a rolling [pin]*, but first Sprinkle it well with wine vineger, and let it lye so one houre or two more, after joynt it in every joynt, and season it as you doe a red deare and let it lye in the seasoning 12 houres, and make a deep square pye of course paste and lay in your meat with good store of butter, and strew on it a litle more of the Seasoning under and over it, and let it bake six or seven houres, then serve it hott or cold as you like, if you serve it hott, a litle thinne

---

* Supplied.

Gallendine of Claret wine, breadcrummes, ginger cinnamon and a litle sugar, stirre them well together untill the shugar be melted; open the pye poure in a good deale or most of the butter, and put a litle of that butter into the Gallendine, then poure your Gallendine upon the meate and so serve it.

72.   *To fry a loine of veal.*

Cut a loyne of veale in thinne slices, and beat it with the backe of a cleaver, frye it in a pan untill it be somewhat browne in butter, then put away the butter you frye it withall, put the meat into the Pan againe, put to it strong broath, Onyons Capers toppes of Thyme, sorrell a litle cutt, Anchoves a litle cutt with pepper nutmegs and salt, hold it over the fire and stirre all the things together, then put in Vineger, minced Lemmon, serve it away upon sopps.

73.   *Fricassy a calves head.*

Take a Calves head half boile it in water, and salt, then take it out and bone it, & cutt it in thin slices, and putt it into a frying pan with the braines and eyes, and fry it with fresh butter, when it is fried enough take out the butter and put in a quarter of a Pinte of Creame mingled with three spoonefulls of verdjuice, and three Spoonefulles of claret wine, and halfe a nutmeg sliced thinne; and if it be at the tyme of the yeare a few green Grapes bruised, and serve it in. [Sr. Ed. Stowell]¶

74.   *fry'd hartic.*

Take 4 hartichokes, cut of all the Leaves, then cutt the Bottoms in litle peices as big as a great walnutt, put them into a frying pan with

---

¶ Marginal note. When Evelyn was in Paris in 1651, he was visited by a party of noblemen, headed by Lords Strafford and Ossory, including Sir Edward Stawell. They talked 'upon severall subjects'. Stawell was of a valiant royalist family, one of whom undertook the defence of Taunton in the civil wars.

some fresh butter, and fry them till they be enough, the which you shall know by their being soft, then frye some parsley with them that it may be onely [be]* crisp; so serve them in with parsley upon them.

75.   Souc'd pig or turkey.

Take a fatt pigg of a moneth old, scald it and gutt it, then cutt off the head close by the eares, and the feet, cutt it in the midle and bone it, then lay one side upon another and sprinkle a litle mace and salt betwixt, then rowlle it up as you doe brawne and bind it with filletting, or sowce it in a Cloth. To two pigs you must take three pintes of white wine and a pinte of water, put in a handfull of salt, a pennyworth of mace, a pennyworth of cloves, and a whole nutmeg, boile it till you may put a knife through it, then take it off, and let it stand a night or a day in souce, and so eat it with vineger.

76.   A quaking pudding.

Take eight egges a pinte of creame, 4 spoonefulls of flower, a nutmeg a litle rosewater, a quantity of sugar you thinke fitt, wett the cloath you intend to boile it in, then floure it and let it boile two houres.

77.   Oysters stewed.

Take the meat of oysters picke and wash them very cleane, and put them in a dish, a beare glasse of white wine, a quarter of a glasse of wine vineger, 6 cloves and a nutmeg cut in peices, an onyon or two, a litle whole pepper, when they are enough take them off the fire put in a quarter of a pound of fresh butter, having poured out halfe the Licquor, and taken out all the onyon and the spice, then cover them with a dish and a cloath, and beat the butter in them till it be quite melted, then lay the oysters in a dish, and Poure the thickest of the liquid upon them, and so serve them.

---

* Repeated in error.

78. *Loaves Buttered.*

Take 3 quartes of new milke, and put in as much runnett as will turne
it like a Cheese, wring the whay cleane from it through a Cloath,
then stampe your curds very fine in a stone morter, put into them six
yolkes of egges and one white, a handfull of grated bread and halfe
a handfull of Flower, a litle salt mingle them well together then rolle
them with you hands into litle Loaves, and sett them on a Butterd
Paper, and wash the toppes over with the yolke of an egge, and a litle
beere beat together. 3 quarters of an houre will bake them in a quicke
oven, take halfe a pound of butter, 5 spoonefulls of Rosewater 1/2 a
nutmeg sliced thin, a litle sugar, set this on a quicke fire and stirre
it continually till it be melted, then draw your Loaves and cutt off
your toppes, stirre up the Crumme and powre in the butter, and serve
them in upon a plate.

78[bis]. *A thistle sallade.*

Take the Long stalke in the midle of the leaf of the great thistle when
they be young. Scrape them and wash them then boyle them in water
and Salt, and when they be very tender take them up, and lay them
in a dish to draine. Then Creame butter very thicke, and put the
water from them, and poure the butter on them, and serve them up
in the Roome of Asparagus.[*]

79. *Puffes.*

Take a quart of new milke turne it with runnett, when it is come
whey is, breake your Curd and pour into it two yolkes of egges, and
three whites, a litle salt, and as much flowre as you can take up
betwixt your finger and your thumb at 4 tymes, mingle all them very
well together, then take halfe a pound of Butter, and when it is very
hott put them into a Frying pan in litle Rolles the fashion of Skerritts

---

[*] Compare to the receipt in *Acetaria*.

and when they are enough, on one side, turne them with your knife
on the other, this doe till all the stuffe be fryed, in the meane tyme
have butter sugar and rosewater in a dish, and put them in as they
come out, and so serve them up.

80.   Cheesecakes.

Take a quart of Creame sett it on the fire and take 12 egges, and two
yolkes, beat them very well put them into the skillet to the Cream,
stirring it continually till it Curdles then take it off and put it into an
earthen pan or silver bason, and put to it whilst it is hott a quarter of
a pound of Currans plumpt, halfe a quarter of Butter, a quarter of
Sugar and a nutmeg sliced thin, for the Last take a quart of the finest
flower, and as much Cold water as will make it paste, then pull it
severell tymes in Litle Pieces, and beate it every tyme with a rowling
pin, then divide your paste into six parts roulle them out very thin
and cutt them round and lay litle peices of butter round about them,
then turne them up once againe, and doe the like, then turne them up
and put in the mesur they must be baked pale, if you make them right
it will make just six. Lady Hattons.[*]

81.   A Cake. very light but not rich – good[†]

Take halfe a pecke of flowre, and a pinte of yeast, then take a pinte
of Creame, and 2 pound of butter, and a tumbler of Sacke, then take

---

[*] This may be Baroness Elizabeth Hatton (d.1672), wife of Christopher Hatton,
first Baron Hatton (1605?–1670), comptroller of the royal household 1643–6,
exiled in Paris 1648–56. While Lord Hatton was in Paris, he stayed with
Evelyn's father-in-law. Lady Hatton remained in England for a time, Evelyn
visiting her on 4 July 1649, but was living in Paris when he called on her in
October of the following year. Evelyn visited their country seat , Kirby Hall in
Northamptonshire, in 1654: 'the avenue was ungraceful and the seate naked.'
Equally, Evelyn was connected by cousinage to other Hattons, one of whom,
Richard, was a serjeant-at-law and close to Evelyn in his younger days. Although
they did not bear a title, this receipt may come from that source.
[†] Subsequent annotation.

the creame butter and sacke, and sett them on the fire but not to boile, then take the yeast, and put to it your flowre, with nutmeg cinnamon & mace, but you must searce it before you put it into your flower, then put y^r Creame to it, mingling it with 3 pounds of Currans, and so make it up. halfe a pound of sugar mingled with the spice and flower.[†]

82. *Sullibub.*

Take a quart of white wine milke as much Curd as the wine will make, takeing it still off as it riseth, then take some of the Curds and lay all on a Row in the bottome of the pott you will serve it in, and on that two or three spoonefulls of sweet creame, and Sugar then upon that a Row of Curd and another of creame and sugar, and last of all a litle Creame and Sugar, stirre it well together, and let it stand two or three houres, or longer a day or a night, you may keep it, and it will be the better, season the Drinke with sugar, and serve it by itselfe. La. Grayes.[*]

83. *Creame Caudell.*

Take 2 spoonefulls of sacke, and one of beare, let it stand on the fire till it boiles, then put into it halfe a pint of Creame and a spoonefull of Sugar, stirring it till it boyles, then take it off the fire for it is enough; this is but for one mesre, if you will have more you must double your quantity.

84. *Creame tarts.*

Take 2 quarts of flower, a quarterne and halfe of butter, halfe a pinte

---

[†] The last sentence was added subsequently.

[*] i.e. La[dy] Graye[']s. The identity is uncertain. It would be pleasingif there was some connection with Elizabeth Grey, Countess of Kent (d. 1651), erstwhile employer of Robert May, and posthumously an author of a cookery book herself. JE was related to the 11th Earl, whose grandmother was an Evelyn, and this may be the link to the recipe. He records a visit from Anthony, the 11th Earl, and his Countess on 3rd May, 1664.

of creame, the yolke of an egge, mingle the butter and the flowre cold, then knead your paste up with cold water, devide this paste for 3 tarts, then take the fairest pippins, pare, quarter them and core them, then with a very litle Iron made in the shape of a Larding iron draw litle slices of Orrenges through the quarters of the Apples, three or 4 in every quarter, you must first boile your orrenge peele in two Severall waters so take away the bitternesse, then cutt the orrenge peele into thin shreds, an inch long the bigness of a pin, then lay them in quarters in your tarts, and put but so much sugar to them as you thinke will keep them moist; heat your oven indifferently, when they have stood in halfe and houre, draw them, and cutt open the lidds, and poure in your creame. You must take 2 quarts of creame; the yolkes of eight egges, breake them every one severally into a Spoone; cut it with a knife in the spoone, and you shall see a skin which conteyeneth the yolke, that take away, beat your yolkes well together, put them into the creame cold, then sett them on the firre stirring the Creame till it be scalded then take it off, and put in so much sugar as will make it sweet, if you will have any muske or Amber you may put it in, when you put in the Sugar you must let them stand in the oven almost halfe and houre after you have put in the creame. If you would ice them you must doe it when you draw them to put your Creame in, with the white of an egg beat very well and rosewater, wash the Lids over with a feather, then searce fine Sugar thin over them, the tarts must be drawne three hours before you eate them.

85. *Sasages.*

Take a legge of veale, cutt off the fatt cleane, then shred it as fine as you can, and shred two pound of beefe suett as fine, and mingle them together with a good handfull of sage shred small and the yolkes of 8 egges and 2 whites, halfe an ounce of pepper, two nutmegs and season it with Salt to your owne taste, then rolle them up like sawsages, that Length and thickness, and frey them with butter.

86.   Barley creame.

Take a handfull of french Barley, lay it in water all night then boile it in two or three waters, then take a quart of water and a handfull of Strawberry leaves, as much of Sorrell leaves and so much of succory leaves, and boile them taking the barly out of the last water. Boile the water with the aforesaid herbes till one quarter be consumed, then take out the barly and stampe it with a handfull of blanched Almonds, straine it with the Barley water till it be as thicke as Creame, and then a litle boile it with a few mace sugar and rose-water.

87.   Curranscakes.

Take a pound of fine floure dried, and six ounces of Sugar, as much butter, halfe a nutmeg , a litle Cinnamon, 4 or 5 cloves beaten small, and a litle salt, mingle them all together then temper it up with 2 yolkes of egges, one white, and as much Creame as will make it into a tender paste, which must be rolled out thinne, then plump your Currans, in a litle water mixed with rosewater what quantity you please, and a litle Sugar onely to quicken the Currans, so put them of thicknesse you please, the oven must not be much hotter then it is after the drawing a good Batch of bread.

88.   Liver pudding.

[This recipe is frequently amended, the interlineal comments are in square brackets.] Take halfe a pecke of flower and of the fatte [of the Smal gutts , ...* & ye fatt end] of the Belly pieces of the hog and the Liver, [and take off the skin] boile them both together, when boiled

---

* There is an illegible word here.

74

choppe it very small and mingle it with the floures, then take the [boyled] Liver, and crumme it [rubb it betweene y^r hands] & sift it very fine, putting [& mingling] it likewise to the Fatt [so tender so as it will not be seene in ye puddings] and flowre, then take a pretty quantity of Carraway seeds bruised with some Cloves mace, nutmeg beaten all fine together, a pretty deale of Salt, the yolkes and halfe the white of six egges, [take no more flowre than y^r fatt will well [cope with][§] with a pinte of y^r Liquor] if all this do not well moisten it, take some [more] of the Liquor you boile the fatt in, and put it, then [worke it to a paste & so roule it out] fille the great guttes & boile them. These we call folkes puddings,[†] in Surry.

89.   *Fine hogs pudding.*

Take a gallon of grated bread, 16 egges well beaten and strained, three lbs[*] beef suet small minced, a pound of marrow, a lb and a half or 2 lbs of Currans, a pound of sweet almonds beaten very fine, with 12 spoonefulls of rosewater, halfe a pound of Dates cut small, halfe a pound of sugar, some Ambergrece, an ounce of Cinnamon broken and searced, a quart of good cream, some salt, mixt these together and fill the gutts with it, tying them up well, and when your water boils put in your puddings and boile them well. Wotton receipt[¶]

90.   *Oglio spanish.*

Take 3 or 4 pounds of beefe halfe a pound of Bacon, and as much porke, a necke of mutton, a knucke[‡] of veale and a pullet or instead thereof 2 or three pigeons, or both; boile them together in a great pipkin, with such proportion of water as make your Broath good,

---

§ Words supplied for clarity.

† Receipt 236 is a variant form of the same recipe.

* The note of quantity, 'three lbs', is written in a different hand.

¶ As the preceding recipe, this comes from the Evelyn family home.

‡ Knucke is a shortening of knuckle (*OED*).

halfe a pinte of pease; let all these boile together with some salt: halfe an houre before you send up dynner, putt in a quarter of a curled Cabbage (not colliflower), a race of ginger cut in quarters, a nutmeg a dozen cloves, as many pepper Cornes, 2 or 3 turneps, let them boile together till dynner goes up then add a pennyworth of saffron mixt with the liquour, serve it all up in a great Charger, ware that the beefe should be boiled more then the rest till tender. The beef is not serv'd up at great feaste. Lord Ambassad. Hoptons[§] receipt.

91. Bisk. French.

Take halfe a dozen or a doz. of young pigeons of a weeke old, four sweetbreds of veale, a dozen of Cockscombs, as many lambstones, boile them reasonably tender in an ordinary bouillon or broath, then take a peice of beefe, of Leane mutton, & a fillet of beefe, roast these halfe, then take them off, and presse out their Juice & gravy into a dish which reserve to powre into so much of your former Liquour or broath as will fill a handsome dish, in which you must stew your pigeons, Sweetbreads, Cockscombs, and Lambstones with halfe a doz: good peices of marrow, which should be stewing about an halfe an houre before you serve up dynner to these you must adde two handfulls of mushrooms prepared as hereafter, and stewed in the Liquour at the same tyme with the other when also throw in an handfull of green pistaccios then serve it up, upon sippetts of manchett which have been roasted crispe by a quick fire.

Preparation of the Mushrooms before they be used

Choose small firme white mushrooms such as groe in the dryest

---

§ Sir Arthur Hopton (1588?–1650) was first secretary to Lord Cottington's embassy in Spain in 1628 and subsequently ambassador himself from 1638 until 1649. He was in London in the latter year, and Evelyn records visiting him in London on 7th June, 'a most excellent person'.

unshady sweet pasture grounds, neither under nor on trees, peele off their upper Shiny white skin and paring away their lower blacke spungy part slice them in quarters and throw them into water, there let them a litle while cleane, then boile them in quarters and throw them in fresh water with a litle fresh butter in it, let them thus boile a full houre (for this takes away all their malignity), then shift them into another fresh water and butter and boile them as before till they become tender enough, then take them out of the water and put to them as much of your Liquor or broath above mentioned, as will cover them, then season them with halfe a dozen spoonefulls of white wine, a doz: of Cloves, as many pepper Cornes three or 4 small young onions halfe a handfull of perseley three or 4 sprigs of tyme, shred all these together, & with salt season with them to an [hautgout]* with two or 3 Anchoves, with a litle morsell of sweet Butter to keep them white so cast this Liquor, & all, into the former to stew as is directed. The best French Biske.

92.   *Spannish Bondejo.*

Memoria para hacer un Bondejo.¶

Las cosas que lleva del lechon son las siguentes.

R. Las oretas, las haldillas, de las quixadas, y los quesos del espinaco con alguna carne, y la cola; con dos gironcillos que se sacan de la barriga (alma que llaman): hecho pedazos.

Todo esto se echa en adovo y es desta manera. Vinagre aguado que no sepa mucho a ello en cantidad, y cumbra los pedazos y con

---

* This word actually written here is 'itagou', but the sense is certainly 'haut-gout', see glossary. This paragraph about mushrooms bears many similarities to the instructions in *Acetaria*.

¶ This receipt was contributed to the volume by a person whose holograph is not seen elsewhere in the book. There are some later annotations, mainly translations, written between the lines of the text by yet another hand. These are included in the transcript within square brackets.

ello sal lo suficiente, pèro si a de durar el Bondejo puede llevar algo mas, tambien sea de§ eschar oregano, y pimiento colorado, [red pepper] y ajo segun el gusto. a de estar en el adovo seis o siete dias meneandolo cada dia; en que se hace se llama quajo, y tanbien se echa en adovo lavandolo primero, y les pues de los seis o 7 dîas sesaca todo del adovo, y de lava solamente el quajo del adove y a tomado – y los pedazos se enbuten en el desta manera – Muelen al caravia [caraway seeds] y gengibre; y pimienta de lo negro, la cantidad poco mas a menos y a menester un Bondejo es; media onza de pimienta, y otra media de gengibre y de caravia onza y media, y on esto una dosena de clavos; y todo junto molello muy bien – y con esto polvorcear cada pedazo, por si, quando los enbutan, y que bayan muy apretados, y despues de lleno coselle y centille por en medio con una cuerda para colgar le, y se al humo por ocho dias no azircandole mucho al calor y despues ponerle al ayre y sa buena sacon es comelle dentro de tres o quatros semanas por que no se enrrancia y al colgarle al principio se pone en medio por a bajo un pallilo o ustilla, para que no se junten las dos alforgillas, porque se es calda qes lo mismo que dañarse.*

---

§ This word is interlineated.

* A fairly literal (but with concessions to comprehension) translation might be: *Recipe to make a Bondejo.* The parts of the pig used are the following: R. The ears, the jowls around the jaws, the spine with some of the attached meat and the tail; with two small pieces taken from the stomach (which they call 'alma') cut into pieces.

All of this is put into a sauce [marinade] which is made as follows. Watered down vinegar, however much is required to cover the pieces, and with this sufficient salt, but if the Bondejo is to be kept, more can be put in; also put in oregano and red pepper, and garlic, according to taste. It should marinate six or seven days, stirring it each day. It is made with what is called rennet [calf's stomach], which is also put in the sauce after being washed, and after the six or seven days take all of it out of the sauce, and discard the rennet.. The cut up pieces are used as stuffing in this way. Grind caraway seeds, ginger and black pepper. More or less the following quantities are needed to make a Bondejo: half an ounce of pepper, and another half of ginger and an ounce and a half of

The forme of it how to be hung up. This is a rare hautgoust:[†]and given me by Sr A: Hopton[*] Embassador Extraord: in Spayne.

93.   Manjar Blanc.

R. the Breast of an Hen, cutt off as Soone as ever her throate is cut, then washed and boyled in water, then beaten in a cleane napkin: then pulled all in pieces into little string like thread, and put into water, then washed, and put into a skillett with 4 quarts of new milke, one pounde and an halfe of flowre of rice, and lb ij of fine Suggar hard: a little Salt onely to Season it, then put it over the fire and ever keepe it stirring one way, when it is allmost boyled put in 6 spoonefulls of orangeflowre water, and let it boyle a little longer, till it will no more stick to the Skillett. Then it is put into a dish and kept and sliced like jelly when you serve it up.

This receipt was given my Lord Embassador Hopton[*] in Spayne (of whom I received it) by the Duke of Arccoat's[¶] Cooke at Madrid.

---

caraway seeds, and a dozen cloves. Grind it all together very well. With this, powder each cut up piece separately and then stuff them very tightly [into a stomach], and when it is full, sew it up and tie it round the middle with a string to hang it by, and smoke it for eight days, not too close to the heat, and then put it to hang in the air. It is best eaten within three or four weeks, because it will go bad thereafter. Before hanging it in the first place, put a stick or a splice of wood underneath between the two parts which hang down either side of the string it is hung by so that they do not touch each other, because [when] it is heated it would get damaged.

† See glossary.
* See note to Receipt 90, above.
¶ Unidentified.The reading is dubious.

94.   *Cabbage farced.*

R Veale 2 pounds: hashed reasonable well, of Beefe suet q^r: of lb, of Bacon as much, a little parsly, tyme and 2 or 3 young Onions, shred these all together seasing it with pepper, cloves & salt, then worke or mixt it with an Egg raw, & put in marrow q^r of lb: in big lumps amongst it, then take a white Cabbagg (not to bigg) and boyle it prety tender, then take it and put it into a dish opning the Leaves till you come to the middle young part, which you must cutt out leaving the bottom whole & hashe it amongst the rest of the meate. then put an handfull of this hash in the hollow of the cabbage covering that with the leaves next it, then upon those leaves lay more meate and still cover it with the leaves, doing thus till all the leaves be Spent and closed up in the forme still of the Cabbage, and so boyle the whole in a cabbage Nett. This may be boyled in a pott amongst any meate; Dishing it, putt some of the fatt of the broth about it for Sauce.

95.   *Turon.*

Take of Almonds and honey a like weight, blanch the Almonds and drye them exceeding well, and yet to retaine their Coulour seeth the honey over a Charcoale fire and as it seeths putt the white of an egge to every pound of honey, and beate it and the honey all the while it is over the Fire, then to make your proofe whether or noe it be boyled enough, dip a knife therein, and the honey being cold upon the Knife, let it fall, and if it break in peices in falling it is well boyled, if not, a second and better proofe is to take some of the honey between your fingers and carrie it into the Air, where you shall hold it to your teeth sucking your Breath inwards untill it be cold, then bite it, and as it crummes judge of the effect: your honey being thus well sodde, you shall put your almonds in, and if you will bruise your Almonds first you shall likewise so dry them. Your honey and Almonds being well tempered, you shall put it into Boxes prepared for that purpose and pressed well downe, but remember to put wafers under and about the Place; where you intend to put the Turon, if you will put a litle sugar in it or Amber or any perfume it will be Excellent.

96.   *To preserve fresh Fish.*

Fry your fish being well flowred in a good quantity of oyle, or butter, which done, put it into your pan or preserving vessell after this manner: first cover your vessell with a ranke of fish, putting between every ranke a litle Garlicke, pepper, rosemary, sage & Cinnamon when you have put in all your fish, put in such a quantity of good strong vineger as shall cover all with vineger, and thus it shall be preserved for so long tyme as you please.

97.   *Per far salidi di Bologna.* *

Take 2/3 of beefe to 1/3 of porke; Let the flesh be of the Leg of each beast with all the fat and grislis picked cleane away, then mince them together exceeding small, and let it stand 2 or 3 days in the cold in the winter tyme, then squeeze into the mince meat the Juice of some few garlicks & onyons, and some quantity of sage chopt very small to every 30 pound of Flesh put a pound and a halfe of Salt, a pound of pepper grossely beaten, and six pound of the fatt of Porke, cutt in the forme & bigness of a dye,† all these things being well mixed together, stuffe them close into your hoggs gutts and pricke the gutts with Pinnes to the end they breake not in stuffing, this being done hang them up in the chymney for the space of six weeks, then take

---

* 'To make Bolognese salt meat'. 'This city is famous also for sausages; and here is sold great quantities of Parmegiano cheese, with Botargo, Caviare, &c. which makes some of their shops perfume ye streets with no agreeable smell.' (Entry in the Diary recording Evelyn's visit to Bologna in 1645.)

† i.e. die, the singular form of dice.

them and rub them over with sallet oyle, and lay them in order in a Box, strewing wood ashes between every ranke, let them lye so for six weeks Longer, and then you may eat them or keep them when you please, or as Long as you will if so be they be kept dry.

98.   *To make a marrow pudding.*

R. a pinte of creame and 5 eggs, (2 ounces of) beaten Almonds, a litle nutmeg, salt & sugar, mix them together, slice some white bread very thin (or biscuit instead), butter the Bottome of the dish, and putt sippetts round the dish, then put marrow upon it, and some batter, then more bread, and after more marrow, and so creame to fill up the dish. You may put in sliced dates you may double the quantity according to the size of your dish.§

99.   *To make Creame lemon.*

Take 3 quarts of Creame, and sett it on the fire, and when it boileth take it off the fire and putt in as much juice of Lemmon as will turne it, then put it into a diaper napkin, and hang it up all night, then lay a Layer of Creame, and a Layer of Sugar, till the dish be full, one Lemmon is enough if it be great.

100.   *The manner of making Creame at Soteville by Roane in France Normandy.**

Let the milke stand after it is come from the cow 4 or 5 hours till it be cold, then in a broad earthen pan, let it be putt over a soft fire till

---

§ This last sentence is an additional, subsequent, note.

* The town of Sotteville is now a district of the city of Rouen. Evelyn made a tour of Normandy in March 1644 with Sir John Cotton, remarking that Caen was 'aboundantly furnish'd with provisions at a cheape rate.' Many English exiles were to settle at Rouen during the Civil War and Commonwealth. The next month he was to eat a dish of 'excellent creame' in a village outside Blois.

it creame on the top, and let it stand a while on the fire till the creame thicken, and when it is cold cutt it round about the sides of the pan, and with a thin round large wooden trencher put it under your creame, and so it will fall off the trencher upon the dish where you intend it; but before you skimme off this creame with the trencher, you take other creame of the same nature with a spoone from another pan to put under the creame, you take up with the trencher; the fire must be very easy. the trencher is like a painters Bord which he holds on his thumb.

101. To pickle Cowcumb.

Water and salt as much Licquour as will cover them in the vessell they are put in a reasonable handful of Dill, of Hysop, of Walnutt tree Leaves, and a Little Rosemarie if you please, of each a Litle quantity with a litle Allum beaten strewed amongst them, which hardeneth them, in a moneth they are fit to be eaten.[†]

102. To season Cherries (Earle of Chesterfield).[*]

Take a pound of cherries pull off the stalkes, and pricke them full of Litle holes, then place them one by one in a silver dish, laying under them white bread Sippetts, put to them halfe a glasse of clarret wine, and the quantities of 2 or 3 walnutts of swet butter adde to this halfe a pound of Loafe sugar grated streweing it upon them, cover it close and let it stew till it be enough.

---

† Echoed in the second recipe for pickled cucumbers in *Acetaria* (p. 101 of the Prospect edition). The printed recipe is more detailed.

* Philip Stanhope, second Earl of Chesterfield (1633–1713) was in Paris in 1650, and was a participant in the 'battle of Vanves' outside Paris, with Lord Ossory and other English expatriates, including Evelyn. Not long afterwards, he was a witness to Evelyn's will, and they maintained amicable relations (for example sending JE venison) in later years.

103. To make Mead.

Take 8 quarts of Water to one of honey, and boile it as Long as the Scum rises still taking it off, when it is cleare take off the fire, and put halfe a pint of good yeast to it, when it is cold to worke, the next day bottell it up, and within two daies it will be readie to drink.

104. To make Raspberry wine.

To make Raspberry wine, take as manie of them, to what quantity of wine you will make, for the wine must be very thicke with Raspberries, and cover it close & Let it stand all night. In the morning run it through a tiffanie, and then put in so manie Raspberries more, as will make the wine very thicke againe. Then let it stand 24 houres more; then run it through the Tiffanie againe, and put in a good Deale of Sugar as sweet as you will, the sugar makes it keep, then put it into Bottles, and sett them in Sand.

105. To make Julyflower wine.

To 4 gallons of water put a Bushell of Clove July flowers, clipped from the whites, and 8 lb of malago raisins wash'd and rubbed drie, then shred them and so put them together in a Stone pott, and cover them very warme, and let it stand 14 dayes, then straine it through a haire sive into a Rundlett and let it setle for three weekes, then draw it into Bottles and it will keep very well. it must be drunke with Sugar.

106. A Beatillo pie.

Take six pigeons of a weeke old, six Lambstones, two Sweetbreads, the Sweetbreads and Lambstones must be parboiled, and cut into thicke slices, take 8 Cockscombes and scald them, and peele off the thin Skinne, afterwards boyle them tender in water,§ then prepare 6

---

§ The handwriting changes at this point.

moushromes peeling off the upper Skinnes, and cutt them in small pieces & boyle them in water and butter till tender, then have some pieces of pallats of biefe boyled likewise tender; hash halfe a pound of raw veale, a quarter of suet with it, a little Oynion, Tyme, Sorrell, Parsley and Spices beaten with it, mingle this hash with the yeolkes of two Egges, and roule it in little bales then place all these ingredients handsomely in a pie with eight yeolkes of hard egges, and pieces of hartichocke bottomes boyled tender, topps of asparagus seasoning all those things with a little pepper and Salt and putting a sufficient quantity of butter both beneath and above the meate, afterward cover and bake it as other pies are made.

107.   To marinate flesh.

Take a Leg of mutton or of Lamb, and cutt the skin from it, then rost it, take three or 4 woodcocks, lard one or two of them, and Sticke the other with Cloaves, if you like it. Take 4 Partridges lett them be larded and rosted, take halfe a doz: Snipes, lard them likewise, and roast them, a dozen of Pidgeons the one half larded and roasted the other halfe slitt and fryed Browne, a dozen of Larkes rosted, four teills lard one, the rest rosted without lard, a dozen of Sweetbreads parboil'd and fryed, with some thin Collops of veale, or lamb larded and fryed browne. Then take of white wine a gallon, of white wine vineger a pottle, boile them together with Large mace, Ginger sliced and beaten, some sliced nutmegs, grosse pepper and salt, the Liquour and spice must boile together, then putt all these meats into an earthen pan, and poure all the Liquour upon them.

108.   To keep stone bottles from being mustie.

[Receipt omitted.]

109. To make a Black Pudding.

Take oatmeale and putt in mutton broath hott from the fire enough for to soke it, then some three houres after, put in some Creame boiled, while it is hott, and putt in a few egges whites and yolkes, and good beefe suett finely minced a good deale; some cloves mace and pepper, a Litle fennel seed, and if you will a Litle penny royall or mint, then take Sheeps blood and straine it, and putt in as much blood as will make them blacke.

110. To make Puddings of Wine.

Take 2 white Loaves, Slice them very thin, and a [halfe]* pinte of white wine, with as much Sugar as you thinke fitt, the wine must be scalded; then take egges, beat them with rose water, Sliced dates, marrow, and beaten mace. We boyle it.†

111. To make Taffata tarts.

Boyle your water, and let it be coole, then take a quart of verie fine flower, and foure yolkes of egges, the skinnes being cleane taken away, and half a quarter of a pound of butter, melted, and a litle salt; make it into a reasonable Stiffe paste. This quantitie of paste will make ten tarts, a pound of sugar divided into ten parts will be enough, then take apples either Paremains, or Pippins, sliced verie thin, and lay'd in your tarts like slateing of houses with round Slates, then bake them in a temperat oven, which you must trie by throwing flowre into the oven, and if the flowre sparkle it is too hott, if it onely browne then sett in your Tarts, which must stay in the Oven till they have done boiling and be sure the oven lid be not sett up.

---

* The word 'halfe' has been deleted in the manuscript.
† The note has been added subsequently.

112. *To make French Barley puddings.*

Take a pint of French Barley, and halfe a white Loafe, and grate it, a great quantitie of Almonds, beat them, and straine them in with creame; then take eight yolkes of eggs with foure whites, and beat them well with a good quantitie of rosewater, put in sliced nutmeg, and mace beaten, but put noe fruit in, the Barley must be watered, and boiled tender before you use it.

113. *To make a winter cheese.*

Take new milke from the Cow, and Set it together, with water as hott as you can, when it is readie whay it, and presse it, and salt it, but you must remember to salt it in the milke, then keep it with turning tering* & wipeing.

114. *To make Angelots.*

Take one of your winter Cheeses, when it is a fortnight or three weeks old, and pare it well, then breake it well with your hands, then putt a prettie deale of clouted Creame to it, thick and sweet, and mix them well together, then wett your Chesfat;† it must be a deep round one, to take asunder in faire water, then putt it in and presse it well and it is made.

115. *To make a Chesnutt salad.*

Take Chesnutts, and boile them till they will Shell, pull off the Huskes, and slice them thin, then take the Juice of two or t[h]ree Lemmons, a Lemmon or two minced, mingle them with your Chesnutts, and putt to them as much hard sugar as will please your pallat, when you have dish'd it up, put to it a litle Claret wine.

---

* A variant spelling of teering. To teer means to daub or coat with earth or plaster (from the French *terrer*).
† i.e. cheese-vat.

116. To make chesnutt pies.

Boile them as formerlie for the Sallads, when they are blanched, cutt them in halves, put to them whole Sorrell, Lemmons, grapes or barberries, a prettie quantitie of sugar; dates sliced, beaten ginger, and a good proportion of Butter when they come out of the oven take some verjuice, butter & Sugar, beat them well together and fill up your pies.

117. To make oyster Pyes.

Parboile the oysters, and season them with pepper, ginger Nutmeg, and a litle salt take sorrell grapes or Lemmons, the yolkes of hard Egges, mingle these together and putt them into your pie, with good store of butter, when they come out of the oven fill them up with beaten butter, thus you may take Shrimps or Cockles, you may bake Skarretts or Parsenips as you doe Chesnutts.*

118. To make a cold harsh.†

Take a rabbet when 'tis well roasted mince it very small, then take Anchoves being washed mince them, and pickle oysters, a litle onyon, lemmons minced, mingle all these together, then beat some oyle and Vineger, with a litle Salt, and mingle with it.

119. To make a harsh of fresh Salmon.

Take a peice of Salmon and mince it, some parsley and a few Sives,¶ a litle onyon and some pickled oysters, mince all these, mingle them with your salmon, and putt to them vineger, and oyle beat and some Lemmon.

---

* The last observation regarding skirrets and parsnips must have been placed erroneously at this point, for it relates more properly to Receipt 116.
† Harsh is a variant spelling of hash, from the French *hache*.
¶ Chives; the form of the word was very variable up to the 18th century. Tusser called them Siethes.

120.   To make sallads of Lemmons and Orenges.

Take the Pills of Lemmons or Orenges, scrape them, water them one night then boile them in a water or two, till the bitternesse be well taken off them and they tender, then when you take them out drie them with a Cloath, and pick them cleane, and cutt them as you please in Slices, then you must make a syrup for them of Viniger, and a litle white wine, and sugar, but not too thicke, putt them in a pott, and poure your Syrup in hott upon them when they are cold cutt a Paper round and lay close upon them.

121.   To pickel Colliflowers Ginney Beanes Samphier or reddish Roots.*

Take Colliflowers, and boile them in water, till they be so soft, that they will fall asunder, then take some of the Stalkes, and worst of your Colliflower, and boile in part of your Liquour; when it is prettie strong take it off, and straine it, and when it is setled, cleare it from the Bottom, then take that Liquour and boile it with Dill, and grosse pepper, and a good deale of salt, when it is cold, put to it as much viniger, as will make it sharpe, and poure it to the Colliflowers, but be sure you give them Liquour enough, that they doe not Lie too close one upon another, Lay a paper close within the Pott.

122.   To make a minced Sallade.†

Take Almonds blanched in Cold water, cutt them round and thin, and keep them in cold water till you use them, then take Pickeld Cowcumbers, Capers, Olives, Broomebuds, purslane stalks pickeld mince all these severall very small, then take raisins of the Sunne, picke out the Stones and mince them, Cittrons and orrenge finely

---

* Compare to the receipt in *Acetaria*, which is close to this original.
† Called 'Minc'd, or sallet-all sorts' in *Acetaria*, p. 108.

minced, some Currants well washed and dryed, Candyed flowers of all sorts, mingle all these together, then put to them your Almonds, foure or 5 times as manie as of anie of the rest, & mingle some rose water or choice Clove July flower vineger, mingled with Sugar, so mingle all together to your palat.

123. To boile Tripes.

Take strong Broath of Beefe or mutton, or veale, or all these together, and of that and white wine an equal quantity; put your Tripes into it with a great handfull of greene onions, blades and all, shread small, a good many of sweethearbs salt and Pepper according to you Taste, boile all these together till they be enough, then mingle a good deale of mustard with them with Slices of french Bread in the Bottome of the dish.

124. To boile a peece of Beef.

Take a rumpe of Beefe three dayes powdered, boyle it till it be halfe enough in water, then take it out of that pott, and putt it in a lesser with as much Liquour as is needfull to boile it enough, which must be half that it was boiled in, and half white wine, putt into it Carretts, turneps, Colliflowers, green onyons, sweet herbes, Lettice, Spinage, and sorrell, boile all these together till the beefe be enough, then take up the Beefe, poure the Liquour through a Cullender, that you may take up the herbes and chop them small, then cutt and mingle with them pickeld Cowcumbers, broome buddes and Capers, then mingle all these with the Liquour it wass boiled in; if it be not sharpe enough putt to it white wine vineger and a good Peece of Butter, and so lay your Beefe in the dish with Slices of french Bread, so poure the Liquour upon it and send it up.

125. To dresse an ele. to stew it.

Cutt him into Pieces, about 4 inches a peice, scarrifie them being well salted in a dish, and vineger powred on it, put it into white wine fiercely boyleing, with a great handfull of Striped tyme, the best part of an ounce of grosse pepper; two onyons, when it is well boyled, putt some butter into the Skillet and shaking it well together, put it into a dish, to which you must squeeze a Lemmon.

126. To make red sacke.

Take 5 gallons of the best malago sacke and putt into it half a pecke of Clove July flowers all the whites cutt off, you may keep it as long as you will it is a great Cordiall.

127. To make Cracknells.*

Take a pound of sugar finely searsed, and a pound of the finest floure, mingle them together; take the powder of dry'd Orenge Pills, finelie sersed, mingle it amongst the flowre and Sugar such a quantity as you like, then take a litle butter and as much egge yolkes as will make it into a very Stiff paste, then rolle them out very thin, putt them upon Papers verie well flowred, and pricke them thicke, beat a peice of the yolke of an egge with a litle rose or orenge flowre water, and wash them verie well over, and bake them in a slow oven before they be too hard raise them from your Paper, and then put them in againe to harden keep them neere the fire.‡

---

* Related to the French craquelins. See Hess, pp.155–6 for a discussion of cracknells.
‡ Receipt 127 is the last to be written in the ornate clerkly hand that may be identified with that of Richard Hoare, Evelyn's amanuensis. Hereafter, the holographs are varied, and less legible.

128. *Wotton Alle.*¶

To every kilderkin of Ale take two Bushells of the best Malt, and in it boyle of Tamaris, Agrimony, Balme, Liverwortt, Rosemary and Sage aña M.j.§ The Sage in the Summer must be stamped and put into the Tunn an houre before the Alle be Tunned: and these things following are to be boyled in it: viz. Cloves, Mases, Nuttmegg, Coriander & Carraway Seedes aña 1 uncia being all of them a little bruised: ginger 2 uncias: but in summer (if y^u please) the spices may be left out; onely the seedes would be continued, and a few hoppes boyled in it to preserve it from sowering: likewise must the wort be well boyled with the foresayd Ingredients: viz. to the consumption of 3 or 4 gallons at the least, for so doing it will both keepe, and be the better. This is an Admirable agreeabley tasted Alle, & may be used in ordinary drinking as other Alle is, for it is bright ,and Medicinal: this I call Wotton Alle.*

129. *Morello or Cherry Wine.*

Take of Cherryes 12 lb of Watter 4 quarts, let them infuse over the fire and when the Water is tinctured to your mind, take out the cherries (note onely, that when the first cherrys are Infused, a quarter of a pound of Suggar is to be put to each pound of cherrys: this onely at the first setting on, & at none of the other infusions) and make a second and likewise a third infusion of fresh cherrys straining out every infusion successively, and in straining, pressing them a little: this donne bottle the percolation in good stone bottles, putting into

---

¶ Wotton, Surrey, the Evelyn family seat.

§ The note indicates one M[anipulus] or handful, 'aña' [of each alike]. See WEIGHTS AND MEASURES in the glossary.

* Wotton ale was relied upon by the Evelyn family. Hiscock describes how the recipe was borrowed by other members of the family, and how bottles were sent from Surrey to Mary Evelyn at Deptford or when she was lodging in London (Hiscock, p. 69).

every bottle a lumpe of Loafe suggar, and also halfe a pinte of white or clarrett wine into each bottle whereoff every one is to conteyne a full quart, & must want a little of filling up that it may have space to worke: thus being exceeding well stopped let them be putt a moneth or six weekes in Sand. This is the very best manner of making Morello or cherry wine, and is an excellent drinke.[†]

130. Beere.

Take a good handfull of ground malt put in a faire cloth and then into the vessell of 10 gallons the proportion to be increased as the vessell is in bignesse. In strong beere a fine cotton candle of 4 in ye pound[*] hung downe into the Vessell will preserve it quick in ye drawing & be yellow as wax when it is taken out. This is a very approved receipt.

[131.]   Sallad. Ashenkeys[‡]

Take Ashenkeys very young, boyle them in two or three waters, to take away the bitternesse, when they feele tender make a syrup of sharpe white wine vinegar, sugar & a little water & boyle therin the keyes as fast as you can possible & they will become very greene: so pot them up cold, they are a rare Sallad.[¶]

132. To make snow.

Take the whites of 5 or six egges, a handfull of fine Sugar beaten and searsed, some rose water put these in a pottle of the thickest Creame

---

† Both this receipt and that for ale which precedes it are written in the same hand, which differs from the autograph which follows them. Perhaps, therefore, both are from Wotton.

* A cotton candle is a candle with a cotton wick (hence candlewick bedspreads). '4 in ye pound' is presumably an indication of size. Quickening the brew means to make it livelier, more effervescent.

‡ Number omitted in the MS. 'Ashenkeys' is added subsequently.

¶ Compare this receipt to that in *Acetaria* (p. 99).

you can gett, beat these all together with a Sticke Clove in 4,[#] and as the snow ariseth take it off with a Spoone, then take a loaf of Bread and cutt away the Crusts, and sett it up right in a dish and sticke a Branch of Rosemarine, in the Midle of it, then cast your snow upon it with a spoone.[§]

133. To make an Almond Custard.

Take a quart of Creame six or seaven egges yolkes and whites well beaten, sett your Creame on the fire, put therein a litle salt and beaten mace, make the Creame milke warme, take it off the fire, put the egges therein being well beaten, put in half a pound of Sugar, then straine all this through a Cloath take of Almond past, a q^r of lb temperd with rosewater well: put it into y^r Custard sett y^r dish into ye Oven till it be some what hott, then powre in y^r stuff & let it bake a q^r of an houre with the Lid sett up: then take it downe for qter of an houre longer, then take it out and garnish it with blanched Almonds cutt in halves.

134. To make puffe-past.

Take very fine flowre, the yeolkes of 6 egges & the whites of 4; a ladle or 2 full of cold water, make it up in a stiffe past, rowle it abroad. Lay sweete butter on it very thicke in pieces as big as Wall:nutts, fould it together, beating it a litle with your rowling pin, then rowle it out thus 7 tymes, every tyme putting in butter as afore sayd. then bake it in a quicke Oven. It must not stand long after it is baked least it drye: if you put in suggar, mix it at first with the flowre.

---

i.e. a whisk devised by splitting a stick into four.
§ Receipts 132 and the first half of 133 are in the more ornate clerkly hand that distinguishes the first entries in the book.

135. To make neates tongues red:

R. ye Tongues and lay them 3 or 4 dayes in pumpe-water: then wipe them drie, and salt them with Bay-salt for 3 weekes, & so hang them in ye Smoke and doe make ye brine of pumpe-water & baysalt.

136. Sack posset.

Take a quart of Creame & boyle it, and in the boyling cutt a Nutmeg four-wayes & take a blade or two of Mace & boyle them in it, keeping it stirring that it burne not too. Whilst this is boyling take 3 quarters of a pinte of Sacke and 3/4 of a pound of Sugar, & and put it into a bason, & sett it upon hott embers that the sugar may dissolve in the Sacke; then take sixteene egges, whites & all, & let them runn through a haire Cive* that the treads & Skinnes may remaine behind; then take the eggs you runne through & beate them very well & powre them into the Sacke & Sugar, & let them heate well together, and then put your Creame unto them taking out your Mace & Nutmeg & keepe your bason still upon the Coales covered: you must stirr it with a spoone and when you find it as thick as you desire it you may take it off and eate it; but beware least you scald your chopps. Lady Cotton.†

137. A good Cake.

Take 6 quarts of fine flower well dried 6 pound of Currance 2 pound of Butter 3 q^rs of a pound: of Beaten Almonds 1 lb of Loafe Shugar. Nutmeg Mace Cinnamon ginger enough to season it a litle salt putt the Butter in bitts worke it well with flower mingle the spice shugar and almonds well together being beaten with Rosewater and shugar

---

* Sieve.
† Lady Mary Cotton, widow of Sir John Cotton of Kent, and second wife of George Evelyn, JE's elder brother. She died in 1664. Evelyn referred to her has Lady Cotton even unto her death.

put in 4 quart of good Ale yest let it stand to rise awhile then have a posset ready of a quart of Creame and soe much sack as to turn it tender put in as much of this posset as will make the paste tender then let it stand to rise Before the fire close covered halfe an hower then work in y^r fruit to which you may ad[d] a pound of reasons,§ stoned and cut in halfe a pound of sliced Dates one houre and halfe will Bake it.

138. *A Tansy.**

Take a quarter of a pound of Bisket steepe it in halfe a pinte of Creame, put to it 12 yolkes of Eggs and 8 whites as much juice of Spinache a little and tansy as will make it greene a litle sugar the juice of spinach and Beets will doe well with the [lome]†.

139. *An Excellent Silibub.*

Take a pinte of sak and put to it the juice of a lemon or two sweeten it well with sugar, then, warme a quart of creame and poure it into y^r silibub Pot to the sack through a Funnell High that it may curdle the better then Let it stand a day halfe a daye‡ before you bake$^#$ it when it is ready to serve in cover the topp with a litle whipt cream.

140. *To make an Excellent Rich Cake.*

Take a peck of flower by weight [which is 14 pound]$^¥$ and part it in halfe then put one quart of Ale yest into one part of the flower make it into a light past with some milk which hath bin boyled and coole againe, then set it to rise before the fier melt 5 p[ounds] of butter with it a q/ter of a pinte of rose water when y^e paste is risen take it

---

§ Raisins.
* This receipt has been entirely deleted in the MS. It is not complete.
† Although this word seems an accurate transcription, it does not make sense.
‡ Either one or the other should have been deleted.
# The copyist should surely here have written 'eat', not 'bake'.
¥ The words in square brackets are written above the line.

from the fier and break it into small peices strew the other part of the flower about this past and 2 p[ounds] of loafe sugar beaten and sifted 6 nutmegs halfe an ounce of Cinamon a litle cloves and mace all beaten and sifted then wet it with the melted butter then work into this past 12 pound of Currance well washed and dried 4 p[ounds] of reasons stoned and cut in peices 2 p[ounds] of Dates shred prety small halfe a pound of Cittron cutt small mingle this fruit by Degrees till it be all in then put it into a hoop and soe into the Oven. to ice it take a pound of shugar sifted beat with the whites of 3 eggs some rose water a litle musk and Ambergreece ground with a litle sugar beat in a stone morter when it is white as snow Drop it upon the Cake in what forme you please with a spoone Draw the Cake to the Ovens mouth when you doe it and sett it in againe to harden a quarter of an hower is sufficient, the shugar must be strewed in in the mixing of the past and not in the flower.

141. Mince Pies.

Take Eggs and Boyle them hard Peele them from their shels and weigh them to every pound of Eggs yolks and whites putt 2 pound and halfe of suet mince the suet and Eggs together and season them as other mince pies. you shall not know it from flesh*

142. A Greene Tart.

Boyle creame or milk with a litle grated Bread or Bisket to thiken it then put to it either chervill Beetes or spinache being parboyled and Chopped a pretty quantity some mackaroone or almond past a litle piece of sweet butter the yolks of 5 Eggs the whites of 3 some currance which should Boyle in the milk a litle suggar and soe stire it alltogether over the fier and then Bake it in a tart panne.

---

* Marginal annotation.

143. To stew Carps.

Take y^r Carps scale them wash and wipe them drye then slit them down the belly and poure into their belies some clarret wine and salt to wash out the bloud then take out the gutts and reserve only the row† have a care not to break the gall then lay them hole into a skillet or stew panne and just covver them with wine putt in some salt one Onyon cutt, a litle mace pepper and two or 3 cloves a quarter of a pound of butter and then left all stew together till they are enough the wine must bee that which is mingled with the bloud[.] you may thicken the sauce with the yolks of eggs beat with the liquor.*

144. To make a Plaine Cake.

Take one pound of flower and devide it into two parts and put one part with a pint of Ale yest and 2 Eggs and as much warme milk as will make it into a light past like manchet and then lay it by ye fire to rise then have 2 pounds of Butter carefully melted and mingle it with the other part of the flower then take ye first part from the fire and mingle both parts together and when you see that they are thoroughly mixed lay it before the fire to rise 3 qurs of an houre. then having your Oven ready take y^r Paste from the fire and worke in 2 pounds of Carraway Comfitts by degrees and soe sett it into the Oven being heat noe hotter there than for manchet.

145. To make a Collar of Beefe. There is a much better reciet in the Book.‡

Take a piece of Brisket Biefe and bone it then gett of the hardest

---

† Roe.
* Subsequent annotation.
‡ Marginal note. See Receipt 316 for the other, better, receipt.

Pump water[¶] you cane, as much Oyle of Machey[#] salt and salt peeter finely beaten and sifted as will make brine soe strong as to beare an Egge six pence above the water[§] then straine it and put in some redd wine to coulor it only put ye Biefe in and turne it every morning for 9 dayes then take it out and drye it well season it with Cloves Mace Nuttmeg and Ginger a litle white Pepper duble the quantity of the other spices and grosly beaten then Roulle it very hard binding it with Broad filliting soe close that not any of the Biefe be seene take 4 p[ounds] of Bi:suet[*] shred and beat fine and strew some on the bottome of the pot which must be of Earth well glazed then put in y^r B:[†] and fill up the sides and topp with suet that the meat touch not the sides binde it with paper and cover it with Pie past washed over with an egge that it crack not lett it be baked with housold bread when it is baked take it not out till it be almost cold then unbind it carfully and lett it lye to coole on a table rouling it some times to preserve it round.

146.   A very good cake. Mrs Black[wood?][‡]. if it had bin given right which upon triall dos not answer[Ỵ]

Take halfe a peck of flower dried, 2 p[ounds] of butter Rubed into the flower boyle a qrt of Creame, [or a litle more]$^∞$ lett it stand by till allmost Cold, take 8 ounces of loafe sugar beaten and searced, 4

¶ Many recipes for collar of beef, see for instance Hannah Woolley or John Nott, specify hard pump water rather than soft rain water. The hardness was meant to help the meat keep its shape better.

\# Obscure: oil of mace, as was used, for instance by Sir Hugh Plat, to flavour butters? Oil of mace is also called nutmeg butter, obtained by grinding then steaming nutmegs.

§ Another way this instruction is phrased is, 'strong enough to bear an Egg to the Breadth of a Six-pence' (John Nott, 'To Collar Beef.').

* Beef suet.   † Beef.

‡ The identity of Mrs Black[wood?] has not been established.

Ỵ Subsequent additional comment.

∞ Words in square brackets are written above the line.

Nutmegs grated, a litle mace beat, 4 Pd of Corinths Rubed, dried and well picked, but not washed, mingle all these ingredients with the flower, then break in 6 Eggs leave out 3 whites, put in a pinte of yest, the Creame, and make it into a light, tender past, like a puding, butter the paper and hoop and lett it bake one houre, [and halfe]§ then ice it as you please [forget not a litle salt]¥. it is a light cake.¶

147. An oatmeall puding.

Take 3 qrs of a pint of small Oatmell, steep it all night in as much hot milke as it will swell or drink up, which will be somwhat lesse then a quart* the next morning add 5 Eggs Beaten, a halfe peny loafe of grated bread 3 qrs of a p[ound] Biefe suet cutt, halfe a p[ound] of Raisins and Corinths together, a litle solt, sugar and spice to yr tast, the spice is comonly Cloves Mace nutmegs cinamon with a litle Ginger, beaten together, mix these ingredients well and put them into the call of a Breast of Veale warmed a litle that it may close into the usual forme of a puding, then tie it up in a Cloth and let it boyle 4 houres, the saulce is sack rosewater Butter and sugar melted together.

148. A Tansy.

Take 3 Naple Biskets grated or sliced and put them into halfe a pinte of sweet creame add 12 Eggs put away the whites of 4 straine the Eggs and beat them with a spoonful or two of rose water put in a litle salt a litle sugar halfe a nutmeg grated, then add when it is going into the frying panne the Juice of spanashe‡ neere a pint, or the juice of any greene herb that is not unpleasant (as sorrell Chives beets corne violet leaves#, some of each).

---

§ Subsequent note, above the line.   ¥ This comment has been deleted in the MS.
¶ The last sentence is a subsequent annotation.
* 'Pint' has been crossed out and 'quart' substituted.   ‡ Spinach.
# i.e. sorrell, chives, beet leaves, green corn , and violet leaves.

149. To make Almond Butter.¶

Take halfe a p[ound] of jordan Almonds blanched in cold water, beat
a q^r of them in a stone mortar, and as you beat them put in a
spoonfull or two of water to keepe them from oyling, add now and
then a litle water till it be as thick as creame, then powre it into a
lawne siv with an earthen dish, under, that the thinne part may runne
through, then beat the rest of the Almonds in the same maner, twice
or thrice over, till you have a pinte and a halfe of the milk, which
milk sett on the fire in a skellet stirring it till it boyles, then have in
a readinesse a sprig or so of Rosmary steeped in a litle rosewater and
salt, to sprinkle in a litle now and then, whilst it boyles, which must
not be above one walme or so, by which time it will gather to a thick
curd, then take it off and powre it into a thinne Cheese Cloth that is
very drye, layed over a dish, gather up the Cloth and tye it, and soe
let it hang up till the next day, then sweeten it with loafe sugar
searced, to y^r tast, to make the Colour exact like butter, mix with y^r
knife a litle saffron, and dish it in what forme you please.

150. To Preserve Cittron. an excellent way.*

Cutt the cittron into 4 or 8 q^{rs} according to its bignesse then cutt out
the meat, pick and scrap the spotts and dried skinne, then having a
skillet of water boyling on the fier, and y^r Citron in, lett it boyle a q^r
of an hour then put it piece by piece into a paile of cold water, have
an other skillet of water on the fier boylyng into which when y^r
citron is throughly cold putt it againe, and boyle it as before doe thus
3 times shifting the water both hot and cold,‡ if it should not yet be
tender boyle it longer, then lay it out upon a thick duble Cloth till the
water be drained from it, pick the strings from it weigh it, and to

---

¶ The comment after the title, 'the best way', has been crossed out in the MS.
* Subsequent annotation.
‡ i.e. changing both hot and cold waters at each stage of cooling and heating.

every p[ound] of citt[ron] take a p[ound] and halfe of Duble refined suggar, and one pint of water, sett the watter and suggar on the fier to boyle, skime it well, and then putt in the Citt[ron] which must boyle apace one houre scuming it, then powre all into a bason, and lett it stand soe a weeke or tenne dayes, then sett it on the fier againe, adding to each p[ound] of Citt[ron] halfe a pint of the liquor of pipins boyled, strong with a litle musk and Ambergreece tied up in tiffany, lett it boyle strewing now and then a litle fine sugar beaten about a q^r of a p[ound] in all, when the sirup is very thick take it off and putt in some juice of lemon then lay the cittron in glasses or potts with some of sirup, adding the rest the next day.

151. my Lady Fitzhardings† Recet for puffs.

Take the Curds of 3 wine quarts of milk put to them neere a whole nutmeg grated, the yolks of 4 Eggs and the whites of two, put in two spoonfuls of sugar a litle salt and mingle it with as much flower as will make it pretty stiffe not hard, when it is so mixt it must be put upon a slice, and then cut off from it in litle Roles into a frying pan, with two pound of clarified butter, which must be boyle or be very hott before you put in the puffs, the fire must be a quick wood fire they must be fryed browne and turned, and when they are soe you must tosse them in the pan, and when you dish them up you must put a litle butter beaten thick with a litle water and nutmeg and sugar on them and strew some sugar on them besides.

---

† It is most likely this refers to Penelope, daughter of Sir William Godolphin, wife of Sir Charles Berkeley, second Viscount Fitzhardinge (1599–1668), comptroller of the royal household. She married in 1627, and died in 1669. In 1674, the Countess of Berkeley, who was attempting to maintain a distance between John Evelyn and his young soulmate Margaret Blagge, took the latter on a diversionary visit to Lady Fitzhardinge in Twickenham (Hiscock, p. 94). This was Anne (1623–1704), daughter of Sir Henry Lee of Quarendon, wife of Maurice Berkeley, the third viscount, since 1649.

152. *The Dover way of pickling samphier.*‡

Take samphier put it into a brine 2 or 3 houres which brine is water
and salt, then put it into a cleane brasse pott with 3 parts strong white
wine vinegar and one part water and salt, the quantity so much as
will cover the samphier very well, then cover it so close none of the
steame may gett out, then hang it over the fier and lett it boyle a q^r
of an houre, then take it off and lett it stand covered till it be quite
cold then put into litle barrells or Potts with the same liquor or fresh
vinegar water and salt and it will be very greene neare the sea they
use sea water instead of made brine, the best time to pickle it is the
Mickellmasse cutting though you may doe it all the summer.

153. *A composition for seasoning.*

Take 3 q^{rs} of a pound of pepper 1 q^r of Ginger of Nutmegs Cloves
and Mace of each one ounce, beat all fine sift the spices but not the
pepper, then mingle all with 5 pound of white salt keepe it drie, it is
a composition for any baked meat, fricassé, stewed dishes, sassages,
or any that requires a true seasoning, venison only requires more
pepper to be added grosly beaten.

154. *An Excellent receit for Cheescakes.* which wee make*

Take 3 quarts of New Milk ren it† prety cold and when it is tender
come drayn it from the whay in a strainer then hang it up till all the
whay be drained from it, then change it into dry cloaths till it wett

---

‡ *Acetaria* also contains 'the Dover receit'. Remember Edgar's description of the
cliffs of Dover to King Lear, 'Half way down hangs one that gathers samphire,
dreadful trade!' In 1665, John Bullack at Dover sent Evelyn samphire seeds.
Pickled samphire (*perce-pierre*) is still sold in Boulogne market.

* Subsequent annotation.

† The verb run (of which ren is an obsolete variant) can mean to coagulate (now
dialect, see *OED*). Compare this toRobert May's receipt for cheesecakes:'Take
six quarts of new milke, run it pretty cold, and when it is tender come, drain it
from the whey.' John Nott wrote, 'Take three quarts of milk, with Rennet pretty
cold, and, when it is tender come...'

the Cloth no longer then straine it through a course haire sive, mingle it with 3 q^{rs} of a pound of fresh Butter, with y^r hands, take halfe a pound of Almonds beaten with rose water as fine as Curd, then mingle them with the yolks of tenne Eggs and neere a Pint of creame. A nuttmeg grated sugar and a litle salt when y^r Coffins are ready and going to sett into the Oven, then mingle them together. the Oven must be as hot as for a pigeon pye lett the scorching be over halfe an houre will bake them well, the Coffins must be hardned by setting into the oven full of branne, prick them with a bodkin, which brush out with a wing, and then putt in the cheescake stuff, you may leave 2 whites with the eggs if you like it best so.

155. *Almond Butter the best way as it was judged by thos who gave the reciet.* but upon triall the tast is the best judge.‡

Take halfe a pound of Almonds Blanched in cold water beat them very fine in a stone morter not above 6 or 7 at a time, to keepe them from Oyling put in a litle faire water then put them in a stone or China dish, and set the dish in a skillet of water to have a walme or two, strew in a litle rose water and salt with a sprig of rosmary as it boyles, then take it off the fire and powre it into a thinne cloth tye it up together and hang it upon a stick to drip then next morning turn it out into a dish and pick† it up with the point of y^r knife and so serve it up.

156. *To make lemon creame.*

Take the juice of 2 lemons and let it keep a whole night with the rinds of one, then add a q^r of a pint of water beaten with 4 whites and one yolk of an Egge straine all through a strainer, and then put into

---

‡ Further marginal annotation. See Receipt 149 for the receipt that was demoted from the category 'the best way'.

† The copyist may have intended to write 'prick' here.

it halfe a pound of treble refined sugar that hath ben boyled in a q^r of a pint of water and clarified with the white of an Egge keepe all stirring in a silver or brasse skillet over a gentle fire till it comes to be of the consistence of creame then take it off and keepe it for y^r use.

157. A trife.*

Take some creame and boyle it with Cinnamon and mace take out the spice when it is boyled sweeten the cream with some fine sugar put in a spoonful or 2 of Rose water and when it is allmost cold put in as much rennet as will bring it to a tender curd.

158. To make buttermilk curds.

Take two quarts of Buttermilk, as much of new milk, milk it from the Cow upon the Butter milk, or ellse with a wooden Cow,† the milk being first warmed, then lett it stand a while when the curd rises take it off and lay it in a Cloth upon a sive the cloth being wett with rose water, so lett them stand and drayne till they be fine then if you like it beat them up with rose water and sugar and so put it into the dish with creame.

159. To make Quince Creame.

Take an Ale pint of Creame boyle it with mace and cinamon have the yolks of 6 Eggs beaten put them into the creame and when y^r creame is pretty thick take it of the fire and stirr in to it 2 Ounces of Quinces parboyled and three spoonfulls of Orenge flower water have some slices of boyled Quince in the bottome of your dish so poure y^r creame on them sweeten it to y^r tast.

---

* Trifle. Robert May called his receipt 'Triffel'. See Helen Saberi's article on the history of trifle in *Petits Propos Culinaires* 50 (1995).

† See glossary.

160. *Eringo cream.*

Take halfe a pound of Eringo Roots and mince them very well then take an Ale pint of Creame sett them on the fire and boyle them with a piece of Isinglasse to thicken it boile a litle of it to trie the stiffnesse when enough put in a litle orenge flower water and so put it into a dish keepe it till the next day then stick it with pistachoes.

161. *An Almond Creame.*

Take Almonds Blanched in cold water beat them very fine now and then put in a spoonfull of Rose water with a little Musk then take the whites of 6 Eggs beat them very thinne the creame being boyled with mace put in the Almonds and when they are well mingled putt in the Eggs lett all simper but not boyle then take it off †halfe a lb of Almonds, 6 Eggs to an Ale pint of creame stick Almonds in the Creame when you send it in if you like it. do not forget sugar.

162. *Bisket creame.*

Take a Role of napell bisket cut it in thinne small slices then take an Ale pint of creame boyle the creame with a few carraway seeds tied up in tiffaney a litle mace allso then take the yolks of 6 Eggs well beaten thicken the creame with them stirre in 2 spoonfulls of sack and 3 of Rosewater and when you take it of the fire put in y^r bisket and then put it into a dish let it stand till the next day before it be eaten sweeten it to y^r liking.

163. *To make Papp.*

Take sweet creame and a litle flower a stick of cinnamon sugar and Rose water lett all this boyle till it is pretty thick then put in the yolks of eggs beaten and mingled with a litle raw creame or milk lett

---

† From this point, the recipe seems to be a recapitulation of what has come before, with clearer notes of quantities.

them boyle but a litle for feare of curdling poure it into dishes and lett it be cold before it is eaten.

164.   Rasberie creame.

Take Rasberies and boyle them with a litle Rose water and sugar to take away the Rawnesse then straine it with thick creame sweeten it to y^r tast and so serve it up.

165.   Goosbery creame.

Take goosberies scald them and straine them into some creame of what thickness you think fitt sweeten it also to y^r liking.

166.   Barly Creame.

Take pearle Barly well washed and boyled in 2 or 3 waters as tender as for formity,* take some creame and as much of the barley as will thicken it then boyle it well have a few almonds finly beaten and put in a litle before you take it of the fire, then sweeten it and add Rose water if you think fitt.

167.   Egge creame.

Take a quart of creame and boyle it when it is cold straine into it 4 whites of Eggs well beaten with 3 spoonefulls of Rosewater[.]

168.   To make snow.

Take the whites of 8 Eggs 3 spoonfulls of fine sugar as much rose water put these into a pottell of thick creame and beat it alltogether and as the snow rises take it of, take a white loafe cut of the crust stick a branch of rosmary in the midest sett it in the dish and cast the snow over it which must be beat with a stick cleft in four at one end.†

---

* Frumenty.
† See the note to Receipt 132, above.

169. *An Apell Creame.*

Take 12 pipins greene or Ripe, or Codlings, pare and slice them into a skillet with some white wine or sack and a litle ginger a litle sugar so let it boyle gently till it be tender then take it of the fire and when it is cold put to the Aple some creame boyled with a litle Nutmeg or mace make it of what thicknesse you please. sweeten it to you tast[‡]

170. *A sullibub*

Take some Verjuice and Milk a good quantity of milk to it let it stand till it be cold then take some sack sugar and creame and mingle with the verjuice curd and then let that stand to setle some time make it not so thinne.

171. *A Fine fresh cheese.* to eat in creame[‡]

Take a Quart of good creame boyle it as you doe for the Almond creame then straine it through a strainer and when it is halfe cold take a litle juice of lemons and a spoonfull of sack so turne it a litle till you see it curdle then put it in a strainer tye it together and hang it up all night then take a pint and halfe of creame boyle it with mace sweeten it and put in the Whites of 8 Eggs well beaten boyle them in a while, then straine it into a dish keepe it stirred till it is cold the next day take downe the curd make it up into balls as bigge as an Aple and put 3 or 4 of them to the creame add a litle Rose water to the creame if you think fitt.

172. *A Clouted creame that lookes like snow on the top and yet is crisp and thick.*

Take 2 Quarts of sweet creame and one quart of thick stroakings boyle both with a litle mace a stick of Cinnamon and halfe a nutmeg let it boyle neere halfe an houre keepe it stirred for feare of curdling,

---

‡ Subsequent additional note.

then take it of and put it into a bason or panne that holds litle more then this quantity, and sett it into a braoder‡ panne or dish to receive what may fall over by frothing of it which must be done by ladying it with a lade† from a good height from the ground, it must be kept in a continuall froth like a lather of suds, till it be allmost as coole as milk from the Cow, then sett it into an Oven heat with one fagot only and that put into the Oven when the creame is sett on the fire to boyl which will be burnt out and the Oven swept by the time the creame will be coole enough to sett in where it must stand 12 hours from night to morning or from morning to night then take it out and sett it into a coole Rome 24 houres more be carfull in carying it that it doe not crack at the top then have some creame boyled and thickned with the yolks of Eggs and sweetned to yʳ tast fill yʳ dish all most full with this creame, and then with a wooden trencher made Round and thinne take of the clouted creame as whole as may be, and lay it on the dish of boyled creame when you are ready to serve it up.

173. The Orenge creame.

Take a pinte of juice of Orenges and the Yolks of 8 or 9 Eggs the white of one beaten very well mingle them with the juice then straine it and sweeten it with double refined sugar put it in a dish upon Coales stirring it continually to keep it from boyling till it comes to be a very thick creame then put it in the dish you intend to serve it up in and keep it till it is cold.

174. The Portgal Egge.

Take 3 quarters of a pound of fine sugar Just wett it with water then boyle it to a [syrup]* and have ready the yolks of 12 Eggs very well

---

‡ Broader.
† See glossary.
* The copyist has written 'sugar' here in error.

beaten with Orenge flower watter and a litle Ambergreece put the Eggs to the sugar and put it into China dishes and sett them into an oven heat as for bread.

175. An excellent sillibub.

Take 3 pints of Renish wine prick a nuttmeg full of holes put it into the wine which must be put in a sillibub pott or glasse then take a pinte of creame and a pinte of sack and a pound and halfe of Duble refined sugar put some sugar into the creame and beat it, together with a spoone now and then add a spoonfull of sack, which do till all the sugar and sack be in, add a little musk bruised with a bitt of sugar or an Amber Comfitt put all this to the wine and stirr it well together then milk a pinte of milk to it sett it by for halfe and houre then milk in an other pinte so do three times then keepe it 24 houres before it be eaten, it will keepe 3 or 4 dayes very good[.]

176. To make a thick cheese in the begining of May.

Take 9 gallons of new milk and one gallon of Creame put it together with 4 spoonefulls of rennett and when it is come breake it well then lett it setle and gather it, with y^r hands then take the whey out and set it on the fire, and when the curd rises take it off you must raise the curd by putting in cold whey. Then take the curds and put them into a cloth in a sive, to let the whey draine out, then work the Cheese curds in a cloth till all the whey be cleane out, then work the whey curd and cheese curd together, with 3 or 4 handfulls of salt then put it into the pott with a Cloth and lett it stand three or 4 houres before you turne it into a cleane cloth and so do 3 or 4 times that day, at night put it into the presse and lett it stand that night and a day turning it often then take it out and put it into a cleane cloth and turne it every day, set it into a convenient place to drie as you do other Cheese, but keepe it in a cloth pined strait about the sides, and as it craks fill them up with sweet butter keepe it in clothes a q^r of a yeare this cheese must be a yeare old before it be eaten the longer you keepe it the better. Lady Burton[*]

177. *To pickle Purslaine greene.*[†]

Lay the stalks in an earthen pan then take as much beare[‡] vinegar and water of each alike quantity, as will cover them all over then lay a weight upon them to keepe them downe and lett them lye 3 dayes in steepe then take them ought[§] of that liquor and put them into a pott or skillet with as much white wine vinegar as will cover them then cover the pott close and past the edges round[¶] then sett it on a soft fire for 3 or 4 houres and shake the pott now and then, then open it and turne the bottome to the top and sett it on againe as before till it be all of a Coullor then take it out of that vinegar and put it into fresh white wine vinegar to keepe for all the yeare the purslaine must be cold before you put it up.

178. *Cowslip wine.*

To every gallon of water put two pound of sugar boyle it an houre then sett it to coole take a good browne toast spread on both sides with yest before you use the yest beat some sirup of Cittrons with it one ounce and halfe of sirup to every gallon of liquor putt in the toaste whilst they are still hott that it may work the better, which it must do two dayes, in the working put in y^r flowers 4[*] lemons sliced

---

[*] It is most likely that 'Lady Burton' refers to Elizabeth (1638–98) daughter of Sir John Prettyman, Mary Evelyn's uncle, and wife of Sir Thomas Burton of Stockerston, bart., later married to Sir William Halford. (See de Beer; and see also Receipt 207 and the note about the identity of 'Mrs Cloterbook'.)

[†] Compare this receipt with that in *Acetaria*. The editorial work that makes the printed instructions clearer is very marked.

[‡] Beer.

[§] Out.

[¶] i.e. seal the lid with pastry.

[*] The word 'two' has been deleted before the figure '4'.

rinds and all, a potle of white or Rhenish wine then after two[†] dayes put it into a cask that is sweet lett it stand a month or 5 weeks then Bottle it, it may be goode without the sirup it will keepe all the yeare.

179. *To make a Bisk of Pidgeons.*

Take a legge of Beefe a knuckle of Veale boyle the[m] 6 or 7 houres be carefull to scume it when it boyles first up take the scum of[f it as][‡] it rises for two houres after season it with whole peper Cloves mace stick an Onyon with Cloves or a piece of Bacon tye a bunch of sweet herbs with a sprigge of Rosemary and a bay leafe or two and put it into the broth whilst it is a boylyng, gett 2 or 3 Dozen of wild pidgeons ready boyle them in the broth about one houre before you mean to dish them take a Dozen of sweet breads not throats[¶] parboyle them and cut them into dice as bigge as pease then take a frying pan put in a piece of sweet butter browne it with a slice of bacon and an Onyon strew in a little flower then put y[r] sweet breads in frye them browne straine two ladles full of broth or gravy put it in a stew pan or pipkin with the sweetbreads sett them over a soft fire to stew, Blanch and slice two pallets frye and stew them allso Coxcombs when these are all in a readinesse gett some [...][¥] crusts of french manchets dried allso some farcemeat balls lett y[r] gravy be made with collops of beefe fryed browne in a frying pan straine broth to them sett them to stew with a Bunch of sweet hearbs and lemon all these being ready sett y[r] dish on a stove with y[r] dryed bread straine a ladle full of broth to it when you see the bread swell put in an other ladle full of brot so by degrees fill the bottome then powre on the sweetbreads then lay in order the pigeons round the

---

† The copyist here made an error, deleted, of inserting 'a month or 5 weeks'.
‡ Supplied.
¶ i.e. the belly sweetbread, the pancreas, rather than the neck or thymus.
¥ Word illegible.

Edge of the dish lay the pallats and Coxcombs the farced meat or balls and lemons Round the dish brim soe serve it in.

180. To make a Potage with Duks.

Take a lesse quantity but of the same sorts of meat mentioned in the other, boyle it as long scum it well season it with peper sweet herbs salt cut [a rined Coast]† or two in slices drie them by the fire or in an Oven, Cut 10 or twelve turnups in dice frye them browne in clarified suet or seame, when they are fryed browne put them in a Colander to draine in the same pan frye 3 Tame Duks interlarded with Bacon 3 or 4 Onyons straine as much broth as will cover them put a spring of baise‡ in, so lett them stew till you send them up, mince some Veale and suet with a piece of fatt Bacon sweet herbs parsley a few beets and sorrell, season it with peper and salt, break in the yolks of egges to bind them together role them round or long¶ stew frye or bake them to garnish the dish with.

181. Rice Potage.

For the broth take a neck of Mutton a Knuckle of Veale a litle beefe a peece of Bacon stuck with Cloves season it with salt, whole peper, trusse a pullett to boyle sett it then scrape off with a knife a scurfe that will come off and lett it lye till it is time to sett it to boyle, then take halfe a pint of Rice washed and picked cleane from blacks and husks sett it over the fire with a litle water to swell it when it has boyled dreine away the water, put the rice in a sauce pan with some of the broth a peece of Bacon one Onyon Coullor it with saffron so lett it stew when y^r broth is ready sett over a dish with bread cover

---

† The reading is doubtful. It may be suggesting a crustless loaf cut into slices dried by the fire, or is 'Coast' denoting a side of bacon?
‡ i.e. sprig of bay. Spring also has the meaning of sprig or shoot (*OED*).
¶ The copyist is here referring to forcemeat balls made with the minced veal, suet and fat bacon introduced into the recipe a few lines earlier. The grammar and punctuation of this receipt are particularly obscure.

it and stove it with broth for halfe and houre then lay y^r pullet in and lay y^r Rice round within the dish and sliced lemon round the brim

182. *Potage Megre or a fasting dayes potage.*

Take a quart of Water 2 or 3 Onyons 2 slices of lemon salt whole peper mace and cloves tyed in a piece of tiffany lett these boyle halfe an houre then have spinache sorell white beets leaves cleane piked and washed and and cut small so put them in, then put in a pint of blew peas‡ boyled soft and strained a bunch of sweet herbs some pieces of bread lett these boyle together too houres then dish it with a french roule in the midle sliced round.

183. *A stewed Broth.*

Take a neck of Mutton cut in 5 equall peeces set it over the fire in a stew pan with a gallon of water a litle peece of Bacon a bunch of sweet herbs scum it when it boyles up then cover it close for an houre and lett it stew softly then uncover it and scum off all the fatt season it with salt and a litle peper whole then take a good quantity of sorrell and spinache piked and cleane washed, put them into the mutton with some young Onyons Blaids cut them, lay over the herbs slices of white or browne french bread so much as will cover the top then cover it with the stew pan cover, and lett it stew an houre longer then serve it up all together this will be good broth

184. *[Stewed Beef & Mutton with Cucumbers]**

Take 4 pound of beefe as much Mutton halfe a p[ound] of bacon put the meat in a broth pot with cleane water some salt a blade of mace 6 or 7 cloves a litle whole peper let these boyle together 2 houres

---

‡ Blue may refer to the colour of the flower: the field pea, *Pisum arvense*, has a purple flower; *Pisum sativum*, the garden pea, a white. There are older varieties, for instance the Lincolnshire Blue and the Blue Union, which also carry the epithet. It is not certain to what the compiler is referring.

* No title in MS.

then gett ready Cowcumbers 6 or 8 payred and sliced a good
quantity of white beet leaves sorrell spinache a few Collombine
leaves marygold leaves a handfull of grapes picked throw all these
in and lett it boyle 2 or 3 houres lay some Bread in a dish and so
serve it up

185. *Pettyt Pates.*[†]

Take veale Poulet or Chicken minced small with a piece of fatt
bacon marrow or beefe suet, season this with salt nutmeg and peper
if you will have hearbs they must be time parsley a litle winter
savoury sweet marjorame and a very litle penny Royal washt and
piked and minced, mixe all together if you put this in past use no
Eggs but make litle coffins and fill them lightly with this meat 3 q^{rs}
of an Ounce of past will make a pye bigge enough, raise it round and
high fill it, cover it with past and round the vent hole put a litle cap
lett these bake neere an houre then poure in some gravy just when
you send them up a dozen and halfe makes a large dish they may
serve to garnish the brim of a boyled or stewed dish, if you love the
tast a litle shallot dos well, minced in with the herbs these may be
baked in litle potipan moules[*] with puff past they are a service by
themselves served alltogether in a dish[.]

[†] i.e. small pasties, which were raised pies rather than the half-moon shapes we
think of today. 'Petty patees' in Phillips' dictionary, 1706 edition, are a 'sort of
small Pyes made of March-pane, filled with Sweet-meats' (*OED*).

[*] i.e. patty-pan moulds. *Moule* is the French word for mould, see also the glossary.
The burden of this receipt is that the filling can either be contained in raised pie
coffins, or a different and more tender pastry, puff, can be used to bake it in tins.
The compiler seems to think the puff-paste version superior.

185[bis].   To make an oatmeal puding to bake (Lady Tucke).[†]

Take whole oatmeal and drie it in an Oven or before the fier, then beat it very small and sift it through a fine sive, then take a quart of creame sett the better part of it upon the fire to boyle, and mix some of y^r oatmell flowr with the cold creame, which stir into that which boyles, so let it boyle together till it grow as thick as a hasty pudding, put in a peece of sweet butter in the boyling, keep it stirring till allmost cold, do this overnight if you intend to have it the next day for when you goe to make it up take halfe a dozen of Eggs leave out 3 whites a litle rose water nutmeg and sugar which put into y^r past, also a q^r of a pound of sweet butter melted stir and well together butter the pan or dish, bake it.

186.   Corrance wine.

Take to every Gallon of Corrance cleane pickt from the stalks and bruised and put into an earthen pot a gallon of spring water being first boyled for halfe an houre then pour it upon the Corrance warme lett it stand so for 6 houres then straine it into a cleane pot and to every Gallon of that liquor put a pound of loafe sugar grossly beaten stir it well together then let it stand to work a fortnight or more stiring it twice a day omitt the last day that it may settle then poure off the cleare and Botle it, adding to every botle one Ounce of loafe sugar. let the corks be good and tyed down while it is in working, let it stand where the sunne Comes[.]

---

† This receipt was misnumbered in the MS. 'Lady Tucke' is presumably one of the wives of Mary Evelyn's kinsman and admirer, Sir Samuel Tuke (d. 1674) the royalist and author of *Adventures of Five Hours*. His first wife was Mary Guldeford, d. 1666, kinswoman of Lord Arundell of Wardour. The Tukes spent their wedding night at Evelyn's house in 1664. His second wife was Mary Sheldon (d. 1705). Mary Evelyn's relations with this family were especially close.

187. *Goosberie wine.*

Pick the heads and stalks of 3 pound of Goosberries beat them in a Morter and to the juice you straine from them put a pounde of sugar and 3 qrts of water stop it up close for a fortnight then draw it out into botles the botles must not be stoped too close for 3 or 4 dayes the goodberrries must be full ripe and the ordinary sort as good as any[.]

188. *an other way.*

some take water scalding hott and poure it upon ripe goosberries and lett it stand some houres then run it through a jelly bagge its owne weight breaking the berry sweeten this liquor and botle it which prooves best every one may judge as they like.

189. *A sort of creame taught me by a Dane.*[*]

Take creame boyle it let it coole stirr it till cold then boyle it againe do this 3 times the last time put it into the vessell you would have it served up in[.]

190. *Rice puding the best way I know.*

Take halfe a p[ound] of Rice cleane picked boyle it in 3 q^{rts} of water till it seeme drye in the skillett, then poure it into a pan cover it when cold, with the back of a spoone rub it through a haire sive then put to it a pint of creame scalding hott, a q^r of a pound of allmonds blanched and beaten fine with rose water, 6 naple biscuits grated tenne Eggs 5 or 6 whites only, some spice sugar salt to y^r tast, beefe suet and Marrow you may add greene Citron and Orenge cut in small dice[.]

---

[*] Who the Dane was is not stated, but Evelyn did receive a visit from the Danish envoy to his gardens at Sayes Court in the year of the Restoration, and did act as intermediary between the envoy and the Royal Society a few months later.

117

191. To pickle salmon.

Take the salmon and cut it into six peeces then boyle it in white wine vinegar an[d] water being 2 parts vinegar and one of water let the liquor boyle halfe an hour before you put in the salmon which being very well boyled take out of the liquor and draine it very well then take rosmary Bayleaves Cloves mace and groce# peper of each a good quantity and 3 lemons pared and sliced the pill† of two of them boyle the spices [basel]‡ and rosmary and lemmons in two qrts of white wine and two quarts of white wine vinegar let this liquor boyle halfe an hour then take the salmon being through¶ cold Rub it well with peper and salt pack it into a cask with a layer of salmon and a layer of spices and lemon and lemon pill that was boyled in the pickle be sure the pickle and spices be through¶ cold before it be put to the salmon renew the pickle once a qr it will keepe a year this is for one salmon proportionably more or lesse let not yr cask be bigger then the salmon and pickle will fill when it is once opened to be eaten it must quickly be spent[.]

192. To make Brawne.

The Boare being killed must hang to the third day then slit hem doune the back bone him on either side cut out the Collers of a convenient size between the neck and hind leggs which may [be]¥ordered to imitate Westphalia hams, throw the Collers into water for 3 hours then take [then take]* them out and scrape them very cleane and lay them into fresh water. Set them by 4 hours more scrape and shift§ the water againe so let them ly till the next morning

---

Gross.

† Peel.

‡ This word is written above the line.

¶ Thoroughly.

¥ Word supplied for clarity.

* Repeated in MS.

§ Change.

at six of the clock scrape and shift them againe do the same at 12 and 4 and at 8 then leave them till the next morning scrape and shift them againe and so let them ly 2 hours then lay the Collers to dreine on a cleane board salt the fleshy side with a good handfull of salt on each Coller lay them one upon an other for 24 hours then wash of[f] the salt and role them into Collers bind them very well, tye them with cloths which have tapes on the sides, and tye them allso at each end let them ly till the next day. Early put them into the furnace with cold water make them boyle quick at first then soberly and constantly till they are so tender you may thrust a kniting needle‡ into them with care take off the scum and fatt as fast as it rises have warme water in a readinesse to suply the liquor as it wasts when they are tender enough to take up lay them gently into milk and water cold when the Collers are neere Cold and hardned take them out of the Clothes and turne best end of each coller downward on a cleane board strew a handfull of salt on the other ends of them and so let them remaine till through cold then put them into good sousing drink.

193. To make a pickle for the keeping of Pork Braw[n] all the yeare.

take halfe Bay salt and halfe white make a strong brine so strong as to beare an Egge upright the small end upward, then boyle it and scum it cleane let it coole if you desire to have it red put into the pickle the quantity of an Egge of salt peeter. The pork must be drie salted after a day take away the bloudy brine from it, then salt it againe, the 3d day pack the meat being cut into convenient pieces, close into a Cask lay a board on it with a weight then fill up the tub with y^r brine, cover it close and when you use it take upmermost piece that the rest may not be stirrd[.]

---

‡ In *Martha Washington's Booke of Cookery*, a rush is used to test.

194. *To make a sugar loafe creame.*

Take a q^r of a pound of Hartshorne and put to it a potle of faire water and two Ounces of fine Venice Isinglasse and so lett it stew together being close covered till it come to a pint then straine it and let it coule then take 3 pints of good thick creame that is sweet boyle it with a nutmeg a blade of large Mace a stick of Cinnamon then take a pound of fine blanched Almonds well beaten with a litle Rose or Orenge flower water then mingle the Almonds and creame well together and straine it hard through a strainer then melt the jelly and poure that into the creame then sweeten with fine sugar and perfume it with a litle Musk and Ambergreece ground with a litle sugar, or steeped in rose water; then put it into a glasse make sugar loafe fashion or what other shape you pleasse when it is cold it will be firme turne it out and serve it in[.]

195. *The best way of making Lemon creame.*

Take two large lemons and squeeze out the juice on halfe a pound of duble refined sugar beat fine put to it 8 spoonfulls of faire water set it on the fier till the sugar is melted then set it by till it is cold then take the whites of 3 new layd Eggs beat them very well with one or two spooonfulls of Orenge flower water mingle all together then run it through a flanell bagg then sett it on the fier and stirr it all one way till it be as thick as jelly then take it off least it curdle and poure it upon lemon pill cut in thinne slices which has bin boyled tender and layed in the botome of the dish you intend to put it in[.]

196. *An Egge Tart.*

Take the yolks of 24 Eggs one pound of sugar one pound of butter the rind of 4 orenges the juice of two the rind must be grated beat all this into a batter[.]

Then take a pound and halfe of flower halfe a pound of butter a q^r of a pound of sugar searced 5 Eggs 2 spoonfulls of rose water make this into a past put y^r batter in a dish and cover it with this past bake it the flower should be dryed a litle as for sugar cakes[.]

[The number 197 has been confusedly incorporated into Receipt 196, at a paragraph break at 'Then take…', above, which has here been suppressed.]

198.   *To make Oatemeal or wheat flower Cakes baked on a stone.* my Ld of Bedfords way†

First sift your flower through a very fine sive and put the quantity of two quarts of Oate Meale and 4 quarts of wheat Meale flower and mix them together in a pale; and take about 3 quarts of new milk warme it a litle warmer then new milk from the Cow and take 8 Eggs and break them together and about a pint of the yest with a litle handfull of salt put the Ale yest and salt into the milk stirr it together, put y^r Eggs into the flower before you put in y^r Milk mingle y^r stuff indifferently thinne allmost as thinne as Batter or else it will not runn upon the stone, to be a Cake thinne enough, you must take a pound of butter and put it into two linen clothes and Rub y^r stone with that butter every time you put on new stuff on the stone, but before you come to bake them upon the stone you must lett the stuff rise in the pale after it is mixt also after it is risen just before you are ready to bake them put in a pint of sack into the batter[.]

---

† Additional note. The Lord Bedford who was contemporary with Evelyn was William Russell, fifth Earl and first Duke of Bedford (1613–1700). Evelyn was not one of his familiars, indeed might have been antipathetic to his opinions.

199. To make a fine sort of bread. Mr Slingsby[†]

Breake a q^r a pound of Butter into 3 q^{rs} of a peck of fine flower, salt it as you would do ordinarily then put to it 2 qrts of new milk warme the yolks of 6 Eggs and a qrt of light Ale yest, mix all together, and if it be too lithe strew in more flower cover it with a Cloth, sett it by the fire halfe an hour to rise knead it very well and put it into a quick Oven[.]

200. La recete d'un grand flanc§ de saxe.

Prenes du mout de fromage le petit lait estant bien pressé jusques a ce que le fromage soit bien [...]‡ petrisses le bien avec les mains melles avec des amands battus bien menues des Corinthe pluches et bien lavées apres quy laisses le reposer un jour[.]

9lb de sucre une pinte de Creme douce, une Once de Canelle, une Once de Cloux de giraffle une Once de Noix de Muscade, une poignee de fleur de farine, un peu de Sell, une Chopine d'eau de Rose une once d'eau de Canelle, un demy cent d'oeufs, 2 lb de beure frais fondu, tout cela doit estre bien mele et travaille ensemble par un boulanger avec les mains nettes[.]

Faits une paste a l'eau, coules le et lestendis plus large et plus long que la forme du flanc un demy doit despaisseur cela estant fait mettes le au four ou ill peut un peu secher prenes un tour de boite d'un quartier et demy de haut et d'une Aulne de Brabant de [...]* pour former le flanc mettes ce cercle sur la paste puis mettes cett

---

† Additional note. Mr Slingsby is most likely Henry Slingsby, Master of the Mint, and secretary and treasurer of the Council for Foreign Plantations, with whom Evelyn was on visiting terms. In July 1670 Evelyn and his friend Sir Robert Murray went to Burrough Green, the Slingsbys' seat in Cambridgeshire, to advise on new building. He was also a fine musician (see Pepys).

§ 'Flanc' is what is written here and at other points in the receipt. 'Flan' is what we would understand by it.

‡ Illegible; the sense is that the cheese should be well on the way to completion.

* Word illegible, the meaning is 'breadth'.

apparrill dessus estant bien mesles avec le mout de fromage devant que de lenfourner battes un Oeuf ou deux pour doner le dessus du flanc puis mettes le au four et quand il y aura ete une demye heure tires le dehors et le couvris de papier pour empecher quill ne nourcisse mettes le au four pour encore une heure le four doit estre chaud comme apres le pain bis ou gros pain pour juger de la cuisson ill faut prendre un baton de la largeur dun coutau le metre jusques au fond sill en sort sec cest signe quel cuit sill est humides laisses le encore au four jusqua a ce quill on sorte sec apres retires le du four et le laisses reposer un jour ou deux devant que de distacher la croute de dessous.*

---

* This is a fairly literal translation, with punctuation supplied.
  Receipt for a large flan in the Saxon style [i.e. cheesecake].
  Take the curd of the cheese, the whey being well pressed so the cheese is well [compressed]. Knead it well with the hands, mix almonds beaten very small, and picked and well washed currants. Afterwards, leave it to rest for a day.

  9 lbs of sugar, a pint of fresh cream, 1 ounce of cinnamon, 1 ounce of cloves, 1 ounce of nutmeg, a handful of fine wheaten flour, a little salt, a *chopine* [pint] of rosewater, 1 ounce of cinnamon water, half a hundred eggs, 2 lbs of melted fresh butter. All these should be mixed and worked together by a baker with clean hands.

  Make a paste with water, roll it and stretch it so that it is wider and longer than the shape of the flan, and half a finger's width in thickness. Having done that, put it in the oven where it can dry a little. Take a hoop of wood between a quarter and a half in height and a Brabantine ell in breadth, to form the flan. Put this circle on the pastry and then put the preparation, well mixed with the curd, on top. Before placing in the oven, beat an egg or two to glaze the flan, then place in the oven and after it has been in for half an hour, remove it and cover it with paper to stop it from burning. Put it back in the oven for another hour. The oven should be as hot as it is after baking brown bread or household bread. To test if it is cooked, you need to take a stick the width of a knife and stick it right down to the bottom. If it comes out dry, it is sign that it is cooked; if it is damp, leave it in the oven until it comes out dry. Afterwards, remove it from the oven and leave it to rest for a day or two before detaching the crust from underneath.
  [It should be noted that the measurements are French, not English. The Brabantine ell measured approximately 1.2m. A *chopine* was approximately half a litre.]

201. *[Portugall Cakes or]*[†] *A sort of fine Cakes that keepe well.*

Take a pound of fine flower a pound of loafe sugar finly beat and a pound of fresh Butter washed with a spoonful or two of Rosewater work in the butter into the flower till it is as fine as crumes of bread then strew in y^r sugar by degrees with a litle beaten mace then take 8 Eggs new layed but 4 of the whites, beat them well, mingle them with the other things and beat it up lightly with y^r hand fill y^r Coffins which have ben buttered with melted butter this quantity will make 24 cakes of a pretty size bake them with a quick oven but not to scorch, less an halfe an hour bakes them some like corance in them

In winter melt the butter with a spoonfull or two of Rose water as for sauce that is thick, then mingle y^r Eggs being well beaten by degrees and then strew in the sugar flower and mace being mingled by handfulls till all is in and beat them lightly all together with y^r hand this way makes them very light.

202. *To make Omelets.*

Take 5 Eggs beat and straine them, put halfe a pint of creame to the Eggs a litle salt and beat all well together make the panne hot with a peece of butter then frye them thinne or thick as you please.

203. *A Rice Whitpott*

Take halfe a pound of Rice cleane picked put it into as much Cold water overnight as will cover it, to soake, the next morning take it from the water then put it into a panne that holds a litle more then 3 quarts, sweeten 3 qrts of new milk poure it upon the rice put in a litle Butter in bitts, let it bake 3 hours serve it in the panne or put some of it into a dish.

---

† Additional note.

204. *Small meath.* very good[*]

Take 12 quarts of water allow three pound or one quart of Honey put the honey into the water as soone as it is warme. let it boyle 3 hours scum it continualy for the first hour when it has boyled 2 hours take a litle handfull of Rosmary tops and two Races of Ginger sliced boyle them in one hour then poure all into a tub or Crock and when coole enough sett it to work with a toast well baked spread on both sides with the yest stirr it morning and Evening for 3 dayes then let it stand 9 or 10 dayes to setle then botle it and stop the Cork down easily for 3 or 4 dayes then stop them hard and the meath will be ready to drink in a few dayes more you may put it into a vessell when it works and keep it with stopes 9 or 10 dayes then draw it off.

205. *Mrs Tinkers[†] Receit of a Cake.*

To tenne pound of flower put 8 pound of Corance well washed picked and dried, the flower allso well dried 3 q^{rs} of a pound of Sugar spice nuttmeggs some 3 blades of Mace a few Cloves a good stick of Cinamon all finly beat, one[‡] ounce together, 4 p[ounds] of butter 2 p[ounds] Rubed into the flower the other 2 p[ounds] melted in the Milk 3 q^{rs} of a pint of sack warmed with 3 pennyworth of saffron, 6 Eggs neare a quart of the[§] yest all the drie things first put together then the sack strained from the saffron the Eggs and yest strained and well beat then the milk and butter bloud warme mix it up as lithe as can be to put into a hoop which must be buttered and the bottom paper allso, then sett it into a quick oven 2 hours will bake it you may add greene Citron and Orenge sliced and wash the

---

[*] Additional note.

[†] One of Evelyn's neighbours was Captain John Tinker, master-attendant at Deptford dockyard, whose funeral is noted in the Diary in 1678. Possibly, this receipt comes from his wife or other relative.

[‡] The copyist has mistakenly written 'once'.

[§] 'the' is inserted above the line.

cake over with Melted butter when it is risen cover it with a white paper to keepe it from scorching[.]

206. *To ice the cake.*

Take a p[ound] of Double refined sugar sifted the whites of 3 Eggs beat with a spoonfull or more of Rose water mix in the sugar by degrees continue beating till it is very white and the Cake baked then draw the Cake to the ovens mouth and spread it equally let it stand to harden a litle while and so draw it[.]

207. *A riciet for a very light Cake Mrs Cloterbooks* way.

Take 4 p[ounds] of fine flower 4 p[ounds] of Corance cleane picked washed dried in a cloth a q^r of a p[ound] of fine pouder sugar the spice one nutmeg a litle Cinamon a few cloves a blade of mace all beat fine mix y^r spice sugar and corrance with the flower drie then beat 12 eggs but 8 whites with a pint of good Ale yest halfe an houre before you mix it then take a pint of new milk boyle it when it boyles up put in a pound of fresh butter cutt in slices and a q^r of a pint of Rose water when it is all melted and a litle more then bloud warme put in y^r yest and Eggs which were beat together, then poure it to the flower and Corance Covering it close with a hott plate set it upon coles to rise before the fier a q^r of an hour when the Oven is ready mix it with y^r hands butter the panne or hoope one houre bakes this quantity, the oven must be as hot as for small bread, Ice it as you do any Other[.]

---

* The identity of Mrs Cloterbook [?Clutterbuck] is uncertain. Receipt 176, above, was copied from Lady Burton, who was a cousin of Mary Evelyn (see note). Her daughter-in-law, another Anne, was daughter of Sir Thomas Clutterbuck (*c.*1627–83) sometime consul at Leghorn (see de Beer). Evelyn heard a sermon from Clutterbuck's chaplain in 1678.

208. *A fine sort of past.*

Take a pint of fine flowr and halfe a pound of fresh butter pull the butter in litle bitts thinne strew flowr then butter till all be used then with 4 eggs work up this quantity tumbling it up like puffe past then role it lay it in patty panns for tarts or on paper it is very good past.

209. *To make Hartshorne jelly.*

Take halfe a pound of hartshorne 4 qrts of water let it boyle in a pipkin gently till it jellyes stiff which put by[†] a litle in a spoone to coole will shew then straine it into a bason let it stand to coole all night the next day put it into a skillet with the whites of 2 eggs beat with a spoonfull or two of Rose water halfe a pint of white or Rhenish wine a q^r of a pint of Canary sack a stick of cinamon a top or two of Rosmary a bit of lemon pill let all these boyle then add the juice of 2 lemons scume it and run it through a jelly Bagg and [put in halfe a pound of sugar some put no wine in at all and when it is halfe cold run it through a double jelly bagg.][‡]

210. *To make Wafer or Hollow Bisket.*

Take a p[ound] of loafe sugar sifted 3 q^{rs} of a p[ound] of fine flowr drie 9 new layed Eggs yolks and whites beat the Eggs with a whisk very well then strew in the sugar by degrees beat it with a wooden halfe batldore[*] strew in also the flowr keep it still beating one way till it is well mixed have in a readinesse papers buttered on one side & cutt out of a folio sheet of halfe browne paper spread the batter on them not so thick in the form of an ovall pretty neere the edge of the paper strew some sugar on them just as they are, put into the oven

---

† The word 'by' has been added above the line, as a previous 'by', written in error after 'which', was deleted.

‡ The words in square brackets were added later, in another ink, replacing phrases that have been heavily crossed out.

* See glossary.

bake them quick as soone as they are backed draw them and with a knife slip them quick off the papers presently clap them upon smooth sticks shaped like a halfe round the flat side downwards close them with y^r hand to the stick when they are all disposed of in this maner let them remaine 2 or 3 houres then sett them with the sticks into the oven so let them stand 3 or 4 hours which fixes their forme and makes the biscuit crisp keepe them where they may be alwayes drie near a fier or oven[.]

211. *A new sort of biscuit. L Barckly.*[†]

Take fine sugar beat it and sift it take the weight of y^r sugar in Eggs beat the Eggs both yolks and Whites with a whisk a good while put in the sugar by degrees beat it still then to 7 or 8 Eggs stir in 2 handfulls of flower put in a litle lemon pill cut very small or grated the oven must be indifferently hott put the batter into a paty pan being first buttered bake it when it comes out of the oven cover it some time with a cloth as you use it cut it out[.]

212. *To make Waffers.*

Take halfe a p[ound] of sugar finly beat as much flowr beat the yolk of one Egge very well (with a litle Ambergrice) straine both through a tiffany then take a litle sack faire water and Orenge flour water and make the batter as thinne as creame then heat the Iron rub it over with a litle butter tyed up in a ragge one spoonfull of batter is enough for a wafer when the Iron is hot put in the batter Just turne the Iron over the fire and it is enough you must often rub the Iron with the buttered rag to keep it from sticking[.]

[†] The Lord Berkeley with whom Evelyn had perhaps closest relations was Sir John Berkeley, first Baron Berkeley of Stratton (1607–78), and his wife Christian, who was effectively chaperone to Margaret Blagge.

213.   To make Beaue Bread.*

Take halfe a pound of Almonds blanched in cold water and let them lye in it a litle while then cut them athwart in thinne slices put to them a few carraways seeds that have ben rubed in a cloth take halfe a p[ound] of sifted sugar put to it the froth of whites of Eggs well beate with some gum Dragon water mix all well up together and lay them on waffers sheets of what size you pleasse let the oven be ready to put them in as soone as they are layed out and do not wet them to much[.]

214.   To make a blanch creame.

Take a pint of the thickest creame put in a litle rose water some sugar boyle it then take the whites of tenne Eggs the treads taken out beat the whites with a litle cold creame when the other creame boyles up put in y^r Eggs stirring it altogether very well till it comes to be a thick curd then take it off and rub it through a hair sive then beat it well till it is cold[.]

215.   To make leach.

Take a pint of creame and half an Ounce of Isinglasse, a blade of mace boyle these leisurly till enough then sweeten it put in a spoonfull of rose water a litle musk and let it run through a jelly bagge.

216.   A silibub without a thinne bottom.

Milk upon verjuice of Cider let the curd stand a whyle then take it off and beat it with sugar creame and a litle sack. so put it into a silbub pot or bason let it stand till next day or make it in the morning for night.

---

* This recipe title is obscure.

217. A Fine silibub. Lady Tuke.†

Take the juice of 4 limons twelve spoonfulls of white wine 5 drops of vitrioll halfe a graine of musk and a q^r of Ambergrece. Bruise this with sugar sweeten the lemon juice with this sugar then take 3 pints of creame put* it in an earthen pot set into hot water then let one person poure it high through a funnell into the pot or glasse you serve it up in and an other stir it round with a spoone till all the creame is in make it over night for next day.

218. To picle Broome Buds.‡

Make a pickle of white wine vinegar and bay salt pretty strong of salt to y^r tast stir it well together till the salt is disolved then let it setle pour it from the dreggs put in the broome buds being well rubed in a cource cloth shake the glasse every day and stirr them till they sink under the pickle keepe them close covered so you may pickle Ash keys and Elder buds[.]

219. To pickle cowcumbers.‡

First wipe them very cleane then put them into Rape vinegar and make them boyling hot so cover them very close so that no breath get out let them stand till next day then take fresh white wine vinegar and boyle it with large mace Nutmeg Ginger and white peper and a litle salt then poure away the former liquor from the Cowcumbers and lay them in y^r pott lay some dill and fenell between the Layers of Cowcumbers then cover them with the scalding hot pickle keepe them close covered heat the liquor thus every day till you see them very greene then tye them up for use.

---

† See note to Receipt 185.
* 'put' is added above the line.
‡ Compare this recipe to that in *Acetaria*. The recipe for cucumbers in *Acetaria* was subject to revision in the errata to that book. The errors identified by Evelyn before publication are present in the MS version here.

220. An other way the lesse greene and are lesse sharp. But mind in keeping.[*]

Wipe the cowcumbers very cleane put them into brine of water and salt so strong as to beare an Egge let them lye in that brine 2 hours then lay them in y^r Barrell or pott with a litle dill[‡] and fennell some spice as mace cloves and peper between the Layers then poure scalding hot liquor on them which must be 2 parts beere vinegar and one part white wine cover them up close A fortnight after scald the liquor againe poure it hot on them so do once or twice more keepe them close covered this way they are[§] not so greene are lesse sharp and keep longer well tasted and are very crisp[.]

221. A Carrot pudding.

Take a topeny[#] loafe grate it halfe this quantity of Carots grated being first scraped 6 Eggs leave out 3 whites one pint of new milk half a p[ound] of Butter neere halfe a p[ound] of sugar a litle salt some grated Nutmeg mingle all well together butter a pann put it in bake it well.

[222.]   Elder berie wine L[ady] Sheine.[†]

Take a good quantity of the full ripe beries of Elder gathered free from raine or dew then picke them from the stalkes and bruise them having drained the juice clear from them to 6 q^rts of that juice put 3

---

[*] This variant receipt is also found in *Acetaria*, although with certain additions.

[‡] 'dill' is added above the line.

[§] 'are' is added above the line.

[#] i.e. twopenny.

[†] The original hand has 'L'; '[ady]' has been added subsequently. Possibly Frances, Lady Shaen, wife of Sir James Shaen, a member of the Royal Society, with whom Evelyn was on dining terms. She married in 1650 and was a daughter of the 16th Earl of Kildare. There was a residual connection by marriage between her family and the Brownes (Mary Evelyn's family) which meant Evelyn could claim kinship with them.

q^{rts} of good spring water and stirr it very well together then put into it as much good white pouder sugar or fine clarified Honey as will make y^r liquor strong enough to bear an Egge then set it on a quick fire in a vessell to boyle and then scum it as it riseth till cleere then take it from the fire and put it in a convenient vessell to cool and when it is throughly coole put to that quantity of liquor neere halfe a pint of very quick yest and so let it work as you do Ale then put it in a vessell fitt for this proportion stop it well and after 3 weeks or a month draw it into botles puting a litle loafe sugar into each botle and stop them well and so keepe them for y^r use.

223.   To make Birch Wine. This is an excellent drink for the fisick and for the gravell in the Kidneys.

In March bore a hole in the tree and put a quill or fosset† it will run 3 or 4 Dayes without hurting the tree if you stop that hole with a pegg you may draw from the same place the next yeare to every galon of this water put a qrt or 3 pound of Hony stir it well together then boyle it neere one hour scum it well a few cloves and some lemon pill may be boyld with this liquor when it is enough put it into a crock or tub and when coole enough set it to work with a toast spread on both sides with Ale yest when the yest begins to setle Botle the liquor but it is better to put it into a vessell that fitts the quantity stop it well and when cleere Botle it if you like sugar better then Hony allow two pounds to every galon of water and in all other respects do as before.

224.   Black berrie Wine or Elderberrie Wine. Mr Slingsby.*

Let the Berries be fully black ripe stalks leaves and all other things cleane picked away set them to heat by themselves in a new cleane

---

† Obsolete form of faucet (*OED*).
* See note to Receipt 199.

wooden tub covering them with some Cloth linen or woolen yet so as not to touch the Berries when you find the berries are heated which will be within 2 or 3 dayes bruise them in the tub and presse out as much juice as you can which juice you must put by itselfe then pour upon the remaining beries hott boyling water with tartar disolved in the sayd water when it is boylyng hott which must be beat to fine pouder before it is put into the water. Then let the water coole with the berries till it is somwhat lesse then lucwarme[§] then run it from the Beries and put the first juice to it and new Ale yest without Hops then tun it all up together into a new cleane vessell filling it within 2 inches leaving some roome to work which will soone begin and last 4 or 5 dayes if the vessell be sett in a place somwhat warme as soone as it has don working and not before stop the vessell well 2 dayes after it is fitt to be botled. to 20 gallons of water there must be 30 pecks of Black Berries and but 6 ounces of tartar in pouder[†] and one qrt of Ale yest without hops[#] the Water Must be only raine Water the same method for Elderberries.

225. Heath Ale. Lady Mordaunt.[‡]

To a q^r of Malt take so much water as may be proportionable to make five barrells of midling Ale and brew it after the usuall manner of ordinary Ale covering it when you Mash it up with about a peck of wheat Bran and instead of hops boyle in y^r liquor six good

§ 'warme' has been added above the line. It is possible it was intended to read 'lue warme', as in Receipt 286.

† Tartar in powder is presumably the same as cream of tartar, the purified form of tartar or argol deposited on the sides of wine barrels.

'hops' is added above the line.

‡ This most likely refers to Elizabeth (d.1679), née Carey, wife of John Mordaunt, first viscount (1627–75). Evelyn was on visiting terms with her from days before her marriage, and was executor of her will. 'the most virtuous lady in the world,' he wrote in 1666. When Margaret Godolphin was sick from childbirth, the ultimate nostrum, disapproved by doctors, was *Aurum potabile*–liquid gold, given by Lady Mordaunt. The doctors had no cure, the gold was administered, the patient died.

handfulls of heath gathered when it is in flowr (which being dried may be kept for use all the year) and three q^{rs} of a pound of good ginger bruised let y^r Ale be with these engredients very well boyled and sett it to work when cold Tunn it and stop it as other Ale. Excellent‡

Dorcasse§ seed is very good in Ale instead of Hopps both holsome and pleasant.

226. To counterfet Renish wine.

Take whey after you have taken off the milk curd and put it in a steine† when it is cold put in a handfull of Balm costmary and rosmary a few greene wallnuts beaten or a hanfull of clove julyflowrs let it stand till it is soure then botle it and in each Botle put a peice of loafe sugar after 3 dayes it may be drank.

227. To make Ice and snow in the Ice.

Take the whites of 4 new layed Eggs beat them a litle straine them put to them a q^r of a pound of fine loafe sugar searced a q^r of an ounce of Ising glasse disolved in Rosewater and strained beat these in a large vessell for an hours space or till it hath a great froth on the top then set it in an oven after Manchet is drawne let it stand in a q^r of an houre or more then take it out of the oven and with a feather wett it all over with Orenge flowr water and dust on sugar set it in againe as long as before then it will be perfect snow at top and Ice beneath it will keep all the yeare[.]

228. An Apple Puding.

Take 12 Aples boyle them take the pulp then take 12 Eggs 8 whites beat them very well put to them a peny loafe of bread grated a

‡ Additional note.
§ Daucus, see glossary.
† This is a variant spelling of the word 'stean', meaning a pottery vessel or pitcher, cf. the German *stein*.

nutmeg grated a litle rose water sugar to y^r tast mingle all together with halfe a pound of melted butter, butter the dish put puff past round the dish bake it[.]

229. A Baked pudding.

Boyle a qrt of creame poure it upon 2 penny loaves sliced thinne the crust being first pared off cover it close awhile then break it well beat 6 eggs 3 whites a litle spice beat cloves mace and a litle nutmeg a litle flowr suet minced very small a few raisins butter the dish halfe an hour bakes it a litle salt[.]

230. A Baked oatmell puding.

Boyle y^r milk steep the Oatmell in it all night to a qrt of milk 6 eggs leave out two whites put in some grated bread a litle rose water sugar Nutmeg grated butter the dish and bake it.

231. To stew a Rump of beefe.

Take a rump of Biefe and corne[†] it well with salt 2 or 3 dayes take parsley sorrell marygold leaves borach[§] leaves spinache and beets mince a good handfull with a pound of beefe suet the herbs must not be minced to small season them with a litle peper salt and white wine vinegar then stuffe the beefe with the herbs and suet put it into a pot strew on it halfe an ounce of whole peper put no more water to it then will cover the bottom of the pot then close on the lid with past set it a stewing very gently for 4 hours at the least save some of the stuffing herbs and scalld them just before you take up the meat send in liquor and herbs with it on sipets.

---

† Corn: to sprinkle with salt in grains, to pickle with salt (*OED*).
§ Borage.

232. *Collops of Beefe.*

Take thinn slices of Buttocke biefe cut crosse the graine of the meat
hack them frye them in sweet butter browne then put them into a
pipkin with strong broth some cloves ginger peper mace a litle salt
a litle Claret wine halfe an hour before you serve it in put in some
gravy Elder vinegar or grape verjuice if you like it allso a shallot
when it is ready to be sent in some juice of lemon and the liquor they
are stewed in with a peice of butter to thicken it.

233. *To pickle French beans.*

Take of the youngest beans put them into a brine strong enough to
beare an Egge keepe them close covered they will keepe a yeare in
this pickle a month before you would use them take what quantity
you may have occasion for in 3 months for so long the second pickle
will keep put them into a skillet with some fresh water let them
boyle a litle till they are greene then take them up and draine them
on a cloth then lay them in rows in a pot and put some vinegar to
them with what spice you like best lay a weight on them to keep
them under the pickle cover them close they will keepe a q^r of a
year.†

234. *To keep Damsons all the yeare[.]*

Bake two potts of Damsons when they are baked fill one pot with as
many of the other as is convenient leave as much space as you may
put some melted butter on the top to cover them be sure they have
sirup enough of their owne to cover them then the butter, Cover the
pot with a paper tyed down.

---

† Compare this receipt to that given in *Acetaria*.

235. Rice pudings in gutts.

Take halfe a pound of Rice boyle it with 3 pints of milk a blade of mace boyle it dry take care it do not burne put to it when cold 6 Eggs sugar some Rosewater a pound of corance well washed pickd and drie halfe a pound of Beefe suet minced some marrow in bitts some nutmeg a litle salt wrince the small gutts of a Hogge cut into fitt lengths in rose water suposing they are well cleaned first fill three q^rs full tye both ends together boyle them leisurely. 6 naples biscuits grated do well in these pudings*

236. The Wootton reciet for liver pudings such as they call folks pudings.†

Take halfe a peck of flower strew some carraway seeds finly bruised cloves mace nuttmegs beat fine a litle salt grate the liver of a Hogge which has ben boyled in Water with the fatt of the Gutts and crow‡ of fatt which when well boyled must be choped small the kernells and skins picked out and with the fatt and some of the liquor mingle the flower to a tender past put in allso 6 Eggs 3 whites the chiefe moistning must be the fatt and what wants made up with liquor round the past# and so cram them into the great gutts boyle them well, after this may be kept in the Chimney hung up they are so sliced and fried when eaten.

---

* The last sentence is an additional note. It is in the same hand as the succeeding Receipt 236.
† Compare to Receipt 88 which is a variant form.
‡ The crow is the mesentery of an animal, the membrane covering the intestinal canal which attaches it to the abdomen.
# The meaning of this last instruction is that the pudding should be made as far as possible with the fats that are itemised at the beginning. If, however, the paste is too dry, then some of the liquor in which the liver was boiled should be used to moisten it further.

237. An Egge Marmalat puding.

Take the yolks of 8 Eggs a q^r of a pound of butter a q^r of a p[ound] of sugar and the pill of an Orenge shred small, put it into a stone mortar beat all well till it be throughly mixed then put it into a dish cover it with puffe paste and bake it.

238. An Orenge puding.

Take 3 Orenges rub them with [—]* then boyle them in ceverall waters till they are tender then take out the seeds and beat the Orenges in a mortar till they are so fine as to passe through a haire sive then beat the yolks of 4 Eggs with a spoonfull of rose Water scald a penny loafe of white bread with a pint of cream mingle all together sweeten it as you like put it into a dish with good past in the bottom and round the Edges of the dish so bake it.

239. To make a white wine posset[.]

Boyle a qrt of white Wine and a pound of sugar scum it cleane pour two qrts of boyling creame to it cover it close with a plate and a blanket so let it stand by the fire 3 hours before you eat it.

240. To make a slight† posset.

Boyle a qrt of milk thicken it with 2 or 3 Eggs yolks and whites well beat a blade of Mace or Nutmeg boyled with it then poure it hott on some sack ale and sugar well mingled but cold about halfe a pint in the cup you intend it should be served in when the milk is poured in stir it round with a spoone cover it and send it in.

241. To make a sack possett with Milk.

Boyle 2 qrts of Milk with a litle Nutmeg when it is allmost cold put in 8 yolks of Eggs well beaten halfe a pound of sugar a gill of sack

---

* Illegible.
† Smooth, glossy or sleek (OED).

then sett all on the fire againe keeping it stirring till it begin to boyle then poure it into a bason cover it close for halfe an houre then strew sugar on it and serve it in.

242. A Clouted Creame.

Take a Gallon of the best stroakings from the Cows sett it on the fire and as it begins to rise put in some creame soe do till you have put in a potle by degrees then take it off and put it in earthen pans into a Coole roome upon the ground and cover it close with a linen and woolen Cloth and let it stand a day and a night put a stick between the pan and the cloth that it may not stick to the creame when you serve it up slip it off from the under milk with a thinne board diped in water that it may not stick so into a china dish.

243. To make calves foot jelly.

Take a Gallon of spring water and 4 Calves feet scalded and peeled slit every one in two take out the great bones the fatt from betwene the Clawes put in a blade of mace let it boyle to a tender jelly keeping it cleane scumed and the Edges of the pot often wiped Straine it from the flesh the next morning take of the top and bottom put to every q^t of this jelly a q^{rt} of sherry or Canary sack a q^r of an ounce of Cinnamon as much double refined sugar as will season it with 8 whites of Eggs well beaten mingle all these together let them boyle all together halfe an houre put it by degrees into a jelly bagg let it drop gently through into a bason and fill what shaped glasses you please.

244. To make Naples biscuit.

Take 6 or 7 egg yolks and whites the treds being taken away beat them a q^r of ane houre then put to it a pound of loafe sugar searced beat them together as long then take 3 q^{rs} of a p[ound] of fine flower beat all a q^r of one houre more then ad a litle musk disolved in a litle rose water warme then butter y^r Coffins and fill them set them into an oven as hott as for Manchet.

245. A Goosberie foole with Creame.

Take a qt of goosberies before they be to[o] ripe cut of the tops and tailes boyle them tender in as litle water as may be, then draine away the water bruise the goosberies with the back of the spoone boyle a qt of creame with the yolks of 4 Eggs beat with 2 or 3 spoonfulls of rose water & sweaten it to y^r tast then put in the goosberies stirr all well together on the fier† and put in the dish you serve it in.

246. Goosberie foole without creame.

Take Goosberies scald them very tender bruise them sett them on the fier with a peece of sweet butter the yolks of Eggs beat with rose water sweeten it to y^r tast stirr it on the fier to thicken and then put it in the dish you serve it up in[.]

247. A quaking pudding.

Boyle a pint of Creame grate in the crum of a manchet put in 2 yolks of Eggs let them boyle a litle set it away to coole when cold beat 4 Eggs a litle rose water some sugar and grated Nuttmeg mingle all well together put it into a Cloth wrung in hott water tye it up Close boyle it 2 hours then put it in a dish cutt it in 4 quarters poure on it butter sack and sugar.

248. To make a puffe puding with suet.

Take 4 Eggs beat them well put them to a pint of creame then take a grated Manchet beefe suet cut small a grated nutmeg as much sugar as you please stirr all well together till it goes into the Oven Butter the dish before you poure it in.

---

† 'on the fier' is added above the line.

249. Rice pancakes.

Take halfe a pound of Rice boyle it with water very tender then
bruise it very fine or rather with the back of a spoone. Passe it
though a cource haire sive then scald a pint of Creame and put to the
rice when it is all cold putt in 8 eggs beat with a spoonfull of rose
water, some grated Nuttmeg, a little salt and a litle sugar, some
flower and a piece of sweet butter beat all well and frye them in
butter.*

250. A foole of any fruit.

Take the pulp and juice of any greene or white plum halfe a pound
as much sugar, boyle it pretty thick then take the whites of ten Eggs
the yolks of 4 beat them very well with a litle wate, put it to the pulp
off from the fier sett it on againe when well mingled and let it boyle
a litle keepe it stirred add a litle more sugar in consideration of the
Eggs put in a dish to serve it up.

251. To make a sallet of smelts. very good.

Take halfe a hundred of smelts of the largest sort, cut of their heads
and dry† them, then put them into a pipkin with a pint of white wine
and a pint of the best vinegar the pill of a lemon some Bay leaves a
race of Ginger some whole piper‡ one onyon shred two lemons
sliced some mace, Nutmeg sliced a litle salt then boyle this pickle
and when it is pretty coole put it to yr smelts and lett them stand 24
hours and cover them close, then scrape them and open them as you
do Anchovisse throw a way the bones when the dish is ful, take the
outward rind of a lemon shred very fine and parsly shred fine two
anchovis shred then take pure Oyle and the juice of two lemons beat
all together the lemon the parsly the oyle Anchoves and mustard

---

* Compare this receipt to Receipt 14.
† 'dry' replaces the deleted word 'draw'; but surely 'draw' was meant?
‡ i.e. pepper.

poure on the fish lay pickle mushrom on the smelts then garnish it with lemon Barberries and parsly.

252. Almond pudings.

Take a pound of Jordan Almonds blanch them in Cold water beat them with rose water and sugar till they are very fine then take 24 Eggs only 4 whites beat them very well 2 p[ounds] of marrow or beefe Suet finely shred 2 Nutmegs grated as much mace finly beaten one p[ound] of sugar part of which you to put to beat the Almonds mix all these together with halfe a pint of creame fill the gutts but not too full the water must boyle before you put them in this quantity makes 2 Dozen and halfe Put in a penny loafe of grated bread[.]

253. Neats tongue puddings.

Take 2 neats toungs and boyle them three q^{rs} let them stand till Cold grate as much as you can of them take 14 Eggs 2 whites beat them well one p[ound] of marrow one penny loafe grated 2 Nuttmegs as much Mace beaten 3 q^{rs} of a p[ound] of sugar mix these well together with 3 q^{trs} of a pint of creame So fill the Gutts but not to full, shred in two pieces of Citron and halfe a preserved Orenge.

254. To drie Neats toungs.

Take a quart of bay salt very fine a quarter of a pint of salt peater one quart of white salt well mixed together this quantity will salt 6 tongues lay some in the bottom of the pot take the tongues lay a row of them and strow salt on them so do till they are all in take them out at the weeks end, turne them if they are large they may lay one weeke longer if small tenne or 12 dayes will serve beat them very smooth with a rolling pin tye 2 or 3 at the tips, drye them in a Chimney 3 or 4 weeks over saw dust or a very constant small wood fire smoake, before you boyle them lay them in pump water a whole night and boyle them in the same water.

142

255. A custard Puding.

First take a stale Manchet slice it thinne as a wafer lay these slices in a deep puding dish strew a q^r of a p[ound] of raisins stoned on the bread some bits of Marrow about the biggnesse of Nuts take a qt of thick sweet creame set it over the fire to boyle with a litle Mace and Nutmeg, beat the yolks of 18 Eggs very well straine out the treads put them into the creame when it is allmost cold with some sugar stirr it well together and set it on the fire stirr it till it is as thick as a posset then put it in the dish[.]

Dip some Marrow in yolks of Eggs and stick it on yr puding and some pistacho nuts picked and slit some Citron you may bake this in puffe past if you please or put some about the brim only it will look well if it rise cleere and is well baked, if the Oven is to hott it will turne to whey and not prove good.

256. A Pennyroyall Puding.

Take 6 Eggs beat them very well and halfe a pint of creame one Nutmeg grated a litle sugar and salt then take a good quantity of parsley penyroyall Marygold flowrs shred very small put them to the creame and Eggs with 4 spoonfulls of sack half a p[ound] of Corance and allmost a p[ound] of Beefe suet shred a topeny loafe grated stirr all well together then flowr the Bagge or pot tye it up close and it will be boyled in an hours time[.]

for sauce take a litle rose water and sugar a litle vinegar and butter beat together poure upon it then serve it in this is esteemed a good puding[.]

257. A Soft Puding or cource White Pott.

Take a gallon of Milk and make it just boyle up take it of and take a handfull of wheat flower and a litle Malt flower 2 Eggs a litle salt mix all together as you would for pancakes then put in a peece of

Butter the bignesse of an Egge then set it into the Oven with Browne Bread and be sure to stirr it just as it is at the Ovens Mouth going in[.]

258. *Elderwine Mrs Bindy.*[*]

Take halfe a Bushell of Elder Beries bruise them put 3 gallons of Water to them let both stand 6 hours then run it through a haire sive to every gallon of this liquor put two pounds of single refined sugar set it on a good fire let it boyle one houre scum it well take it off sett it to coole when cold enough make a Browne toast well Baked on both sides spread with yest put it into the liquor when it has worked over put into it two Bottles of Renish wine and 3 Ounces of Juice of Orenges then put all into a Vessell that fitts the quantity stop it well and 2 Months after it is cleere draw it off into Bottles it is not good to drink under halfe a yeare[.]

259. *To make french Biscuit upon paper.*

Take 6 Eggs beat the whites by them selves extreme well then mix them with the yolks which must be beat also then strew in a pound of double refined sugar beat all halfe an houre then mix with a litle sugar halfe a graine of musk and Ambergrice put it in then strew in by degrees 3 q^{rs} of a pound of fine flower also halfe the rind of a lemon grated or cutt small then lay the batter out upon papers Sift som sugar over them but shake it off againe and so bake them.

260. *To make shrewsbery Cakes.*

Take one pound of butter halfe a pound of sugar sifted, 4 Eggs, no whites, one pound of flouer well dried mix the sugar butter and Eggs before you put in the flower, you may if you please put in some Coriander seeds beat, so make it into a past and role it into cakes and

---

[*] This person is unidentified.

cutt thim with a glasse using a litle flouer that they may not stick to the board or roling pin so bake them Let not the oven be to hott.

261. To make a sort of Browne waffers.

Take 2 Eggs foure spoonfulls of sack and as much milk one Ounce of Cinnamon finely beat and sifted then mix all these together with two or 3 spoonfulls of sugar sifted then take as much fine flouer as will make it into a thine batter then take a spoonfull and drop it on the Irons being hott but not so hott to burne the Waffers, they are very soone enough so you must turne them as soon as you take them off the Irons if you butter the Irons it will be better being the waffers are apt to stick you must keep them in an Oven or stove for the cold Ayre will make them full and soft.

262. To pickle Cowcumbers like Mango. this is twice.[*]

Take great Cowcumbers that are about the size of Mangoes and looke greene open them on the side take out the seeds and put into them a litle clove of garlick or Roccombo seeds[†] then put them into an earthen vessell with as much White wine vinegar as will cover them boyle in the vinegar whole peper Cloves and Mace, put into it when it is off the fire as much salt as will make a very gentle brine then pour it boyling hott upon the Cowcumbers cover them close till the next day then put the Cowcombers with a litle dill and the pickle into a large skillet or pot boyle them a boyle or two then put them into an earthen pot againe and cover them close the next day when they are cold put in a large spoonfull of beat Mustard seed, keepe them from the Ayre when you take them out use a spoone and do not touch them with y^r fingers.

---

[*] Compare this to Receipt 335 and to that in *Acetaria*. The note that 'this is twice' is a subsequent addition.

[†] 'or Roccombo seeds' added above the line.

263.   To make a Hartichoke Pie.

Take 6 or 8 Hartichokes according to the biggnesse of the pye boyle
them allmost tender enough to eat when they are cold scrape off
what is good at the bottom of the leaves take off the choke and cutt
the bottoms cleane from the stalk if there is any left to them If you
bake the pye in a patty pan make short crust, or puffe past, cover the
pan then lay butter in the bottom then the hartichokes cut in halfes
or q^{rs} according to the biggnesse, place 6 hard Eggs either whole or
in halfes a good quantity of peeces of marrow diped in yolks of Raw
Eggs lay some blades of Mace and litle bitts of Cinamon, strew a
litle salt lightly over them lay bitts of greene Citron, Candied
Orenge, some Apricocks cut in slices some bitts of eringo some
slices of dates strew over all some sugar allso the hartichoke that
was scraped off the leaves, placed in patches to fill up: last of all a
good quantity of Butter and the small bitts of marrow putt on the lid
and bake it.

Then make a caudle with a pint of good White wine let it boyle
to take of the rawnesse with the sugar stirr in a good peece of butter
and the yolks of 4 Eggs well beat mingle all by degrees least it
curdle stirr it well till through hott and pretty thick then open the lid
and poure it in so serve it up.

Make short crust take a pound and halfe of flower halfe a pound
of butter [rather an ounce or two more]*, rub the butter into the
flouer then break in one Egge leave a litle of the white out. add a litle
cold water not too much for feare it make it tough work it well not
to stiff this is enough for a midlesized patty pann if you use a larger
add more it is good past for pidgeons and enough for a pann that
holds 6 pidgeons or the upper quantity of hartichokes[.]

---

* The phrase in square brackets is inserted above the line.

264. To dresse a Pike.

All fish in generall is best dressed alive a Carp and pike especially,[‡] scale and wash the pike slit it downe the belly take out the milt turne the fish into a round forme fix it with a scure[†] then sett on so much Water 1 part vinegar and white wine as may cover the fish, put in a good handfull of salt, a small bundle of sweet herbs a litle lemon pill a litle bitt of horse Redish some whole spice as piper Mace and a few Cloves Make the liquor boyle, then put in the Picke cover it let it boyle till the fish is enough scum it well when enough take some of the liquor Melt in it by degrees a good quantity of fresh butter shake it that it may be very thick, then take up the fish draine it well put it in a dish and cover it with sauce if you have Oysters and shrimps stew them in a litle good liquor with spice garnish the fish with them, if you love Anchovis melt some into the liquor before you put in the butter straine it allso then beat it up thick.

To garnish the brims of the dish grate crust of bread lay some tufts of horse Redish scraped some slices of lemon or pickled Barberies. Stew the melt with the pike put it in the dish with it. In the same manner you make dresse a Cods head.

265. A good sillybub.

Take a pint of Renish Wine the juice of two lemons a litle Amber greece and musk bruised with a litle sugar about 2 grains of each. Sweeten the wine pretty sweet then poure a q^{rt} of creame through a glasse funnell to the liquor in a silybub pot let it stand till the next day strew a litle fine sugar on the top when you send it in[.]

put in a litle of the rind of the lemon into the wine so let it remaine all the time pouer the cream from a high place into the pott it will curdle the better.

---

‡ Evelyn constructed a carp pond at Sayes Court to follow this advice.
† Skewer.

266. Litle puffe pudings.

Take 6 Eggs 2 whites beat [and straine]* the Eggs put them to a pint of creame, put as much flouer to the creame and Eggs as will make it as thick as pancake batter, beat it very well put in halfe a grated nutmeg a litle salt some sugar butter as many cups as this quantity will fill of a reasonable size fill them bake them quick turne them out into a dish put butter a spoonfull of sack a litle sugar beat it up thick put this sauce in the dish to them, rosewater in the sauce if you like it instead of the sack.

267. A Fryday or puffe puding. this is twice.†

Beat 4 Eggs very well put to them a pint and halfe of thin creame beat in it as much flower as makes it a litle thicker than pancake batter put in one spoonfull of sugar a litle salt halfe a nuttmeg grated beat it halfe an houre very well let it stand 2 or 3 hours have the Oven ready it will bake in halfe an houre the dish must be very well buttered before you put it in.

268. To make a light plum cake. Oven glased.‡

Take 3 pound of flower well dried 3 pound and halfe of corance washed dried and picked halfe an ounce of Mace beat a quarter of a p[ound] of loafe sugar mix them together then take a quart of thick creame and 3 q^{rs} of a pound of butter heat both on the fire till the butter is melted then take a pint of good Ale yeast 8 eggs 4 whites beat them well mix them with the yest then put the creame to it mix up the cake let it lye halfe an houre to rise butter the hoop and bake it 3 q^{rs} of an houre is enough this is a good sort to drop on papers for small Cakes.

---

* The words in square brackets added above the line.
† The duplicate (almost word for word) is number 272, below. The second receipt has been omitted from this transcription.
‡ Although there is this note concerning the glazing or icing of this cake, the receipt is innocent of any instruction.

269. To make French Bread.

Take 3 qrts of fine flower two Eggs a litle salt halfe a pint of Ale yest and halfe a pint of milk a litle warme put all these together and work them up to a dough, then put them into litle dishes and let them rise halfe an houre, after bake them this quantity will make one Dozen and halfe of loaves.

270. To make Fritters.

Take a pound of flower a good glasse of sack a pint of Ale halfe a nutmeg 4 cloves 8 blades of mace one stick of Cinnamon beat all fine 8 eggs 4 whites some sugar 6 pipins cut in litle square peeces the[y] must be fryed in fine lard and when they begin to be browne lay them upon a skimer and let the lard drop from them.

271. To make Duch waffers.

Take 2 quarts of new Milk or creame which is better boyle it and let it stand till allmost cold then put in two spoonfulls of good ale yest stir it well in to the milk then mingle by degrees so much fine flower with the milk as will make a thinn batter then melt halfe a pound of butter and stirr it in beat 10 or 12 eggs well stirr them in and beat the batter thoroughly then let it stand covered by the fire side if you desire to eat them at night make them in the morning the Iron which they are baked in must be rubed over with butter tyed up in a clean peece of linnen the sauce is sack sugar and fresh butter beat up thick and put over them many chuse to eat them drie.

272. Fryday puding. [Receipt omitted.]*

273. An Almond puding to bake.

Take a full quart of creame make it just boyle with a blade of mace or two slice the crum of two french roles, Blanch halfe a pound of

---

* Recipe omitted; it repeats Receipt 267.

Jordan Almonds let them be beat fine with 2 or 3 spoonfulls of creame to keepe them from Oyling, put them to the creame and bread straine all through a cource sive beat the yolks of 16 Eggs straine them to the creame stirr all together, sweeten it to y^r tast put in a litle salt halfe a pound of marrow if you have none Biefe suet shred very fine strew some citron shred very fine into it butter the dish and put it in, when you put in the marrow scrape off the bloudy part dip the marrow in raw yolks of eggs, and lay it thick upon the puding slice some citron and stick it in let it bake quick else it will not rise, yet it must not scorch, that destroyes the beauty of it if you have no french bread other good white bread may serve in a lesse quantity the batter is not to be set on the fire after the Eggs are in.

274. To make white oatmeall pudings or icings.[†]

Take one qrt of halfe oatmell grists lay them all night in soake in new milke over a few Embers to keepe it warme then take 12 Eggs halfe the whites very well beat 2 p[ounds] of beefe suet shred small a pound of sugar nutmeg grated mace cinnamon and a few cloves beat some rose water a litle salt mingle all well together fill the guts but not too full.

275. Directions to prepare the guts for the pudings.

Scrape the litle guts when they are very well scoured take them one by one and lay one end of the gut on a table and hold part of the gut in y^r hand then scrape it with a knife that is not to sharp there will come a great deale of filth from them you will imagine the gut were scraped away when they are don as they should be you will find them very cleere when all are scraped drie them in a cloth and sprinckle a litle rose water on them as you rub them in clothes they

---

[†] Icing is a variant spelling of ising, a word of dubious origin, which meant a sort of sausage (*OED*).

must be blowne before you fill them to see where to cutt be sure to fill the guts very lank* the scraped gutt will hold boyling better then any.

Lay a dish on the bottom of the Ketle make the water boyle before you put in the pudings let them boyle a pace take them up when they have boyled a litle while prick them and put them in again never prick marrow pudings nor the liver ones.

276. To make rice pudings.

Take halfe a pound of rice cleane picked boyle it in 3 quarts of milk till it is tender then straine it through a cullender put to it a penny loafe of grated bread a p[ound] and halfe of beefe suet shred very fine 16 eggs 4 whites beat them well 2 Nuttmegs grated as much mace beat fine halfe a pint of creame a litle Rose water a p[ound] of sugar a litle muske and Ambergreece fill the gutts but not to full this quantity will make neare 3 dozen of double pudings boyle them quick.

277. To make bread pudings with corance.

Take 24 Eggs but 8 whites well beat one pound of bread grated and sifted through a cullender 2 p[ounds] of beefe suet cutt small one p[ound] and halfe of corance washed picked and dried 2 nutmegs grated halfe as much mace beat one pound of sugar halfe a pint of creame a litle rose water a litle salt mix all well together fill the guts not too full halfe boyle them take them up to coole a litle put them in againe boyle them till enough this quantity will make 3 dozen when they are boyled wipe them with a cloth.

---

* Sir Kenelm Digby advises that the small guts should be filled 'very lankley' when making white puddings, i.e. loosely.

278. An Almond Tart.

Take half a p[ound] of Almonds blanched in cold water dried in a
cloth and beat not too fine put in a litle creame that they may not
turne to Oyle in the beating boyle a qrt of creame thicken it with 8
yolks of Eggs on the fire sweeten it as you think fitt take care it dos
not curdle on the fire have ready 3 Naples biscuits grated put halfe
the creame to them the other halfe to the Almonds mix them well
together put two spoonfulls of Orenge flower water to the Almonds
grate in halfe a nutmeg cover the patty pan with past made with an
Egg halfe a pound of butter a pound and q^r of flower and faire water
mix it up do not wet it to much but work it well have ready shred a
peece of greene citron a quarter of a p[ound] Midle bacon cut as
thinn as paper the marrow of two bones cut in small peeces then lay
halfe the bacon on the bottom so fill the pan lay in the Citron and
peeces of Marrow in the Midle and round about then fill it up with
the tourt stuffe lay the slices of bacon last of all then cut some peeces
of past with the jagge* the breadth of a topeny Ruban and barr it over
do it neere the Edge close the tarts well bake it in a quick oven but
not scorch it.

279. Queene Dowagers Custard.‡

Take as many China dishes full of creame as you would have
custards and as many Eggs as cups put away half the whites straine
the Eggs beat them with a litle Orenge flower water or rose water
then mingle them with the creame which must be first boyled set it
on againe keep it stirred one way let it boyle gently till thick enough
sweeten it and fill the cups this makes a very good sort of a custard.

---

* Jagging-iron or pastry wheel. cf. *Martha Washington's Booke of Cookery*, p. 320.
  Called by Hannah Glasse a marking iron, by Ann Cook a jager-iron.
† Receipt 303 contains the same definition of breadth.
‡ Henrietta Maria (1609–69), wife of Charles I. I have not found this recipe in *The
  Queens Closet Opened*, which might have been thought a likely source.

280. To make [—]‡ chescakes.

Take 7 quarts of New Milk and one of creame set it together with 3 or 4 spoonfulls of Renet set it pretty warme when it is come break it gently with y^r hands then whey it very drie that no whey remaines then slice into the curd a p[ound] of fresh butter rub the curd and butter well with y^r hands then beat it in a Morter very fine with 4 or 5 spoonfulls of Rose water 2 Nuttmegs grated 6 blades of Mace beat fine 16 eggs 4 whites beat the eggs well straine them a p[ound] and halfe of sugar to halfe the curd put a p[ound] and halfe of corance cleane picked washed and dried mingle them well and put them into past.

Wett a p[ound] and halfe of flower with 4 eggs and a litle faire water then role out the past and role in halfe a pound of fresh butter to make it into a bastard puffe past [...]† papers about them least they run in the oven or put them in patty pans the oven must be quick.

281. The Lady Ashleys§ cheescakes.

Take 6 quarts of milk from the cow and put to it 3 pints of creame turne it with a litle rennet then whey it in a cloth as quick as you can break the curd very small put a pound of butter to the curd breaking it into very litle bitts mingling it with the curd then take 8 Eggs 2 whites breaking them a litle mingle them with the curd put in halfe a p[ound] of sugar 2 Nuttmeggs grated a litle mace well beat.

then take 3 handfulls of fine flower put to it halfe a pound of butter in litle bitts and wett it with warme water make the past thinn

---

‡ Illegible word.

† Illegible, but the sense is 'put'.

§ Possibly one of the wives of Sir Anthony Ashley Cooper (1621–83), politician, 1st Baron Ashley 1662, 1st Earl of Shaftesbury 1672. The most likely is his third, Margaret, daughter of Lord Spencer, whom he married in 1655. She died in 1693. There was once a proposal that his son should marry Evelyn's niece.

and lay the curd thick because the cheescakes are apt to run over tye about every one a peece of paper.

282. A glasing creame.

Take thick creame season it with Orenge flower water or Rose water and fine sugar take 2 or 3 large blades of Mace put all into a glasse churne and churne it till it is allmost butter then poure it into a dish and serve it in take care it dos not turne to butter[.]

283. A clouted creame.

Take 2 gallons of new milk set it on a fire not over hot when it begins to boyle put in a quart of thick sweet creame by litle and litle all over stirr it gently with a wood spatula let it boyle very softly for an houre then take it off and cover it till the next morning when it will be thick take it off with a creame dish as thick as you can and lay it in the dish you would serve it in, some put raw creame rose water and sugar to it but that as you like.

284 A fine syllabub.

Take white wine lemon and sugar the juice of the lemon some sliced Nutmeg thick creame put these together into the syllibub pot beat it very well with a spoone then let it stand a q^r of an houre or more milk upon it* to fill up the pot which should be neere 3 quarters full before you milk upon it let it stand an houre before you eat it.

---

* See glossary under SYLLABUB.

285. The Lady Huet's[*] Cheese.

Take to one meale[†] of new milk two meales of creame set it together
with hot water and as much runnet as will make it come pritty tender
then take it up as thinne as you can with a flitting dish lay it into a
cloth so let it lye halfe an houre then presse it gently with yr hands
when it is wheyed enough poure cold water upon it so let it lye till
it is coole then put it into the mot[#] and us[e] a 50 p[ound] whight[§]
upon it turne it every two hours at night it may be put in an ordinary
presse it may be coulerd with marygolds if one please the best time
to make it is when the cows go in Ravens[‡][.]

286. A creame cheese dried in straw.

Take 3 qts of new milk one q[rt] of creame one spoonfull of runnet set
it lue warme[*] when it is come lay the curd on the straw that the whey
may run from it keep it in order on both sides turne it 4 or 5 times
the first[†]day upon an other straw mat salt it a litle on both sides turne
it every day twice, in a fortnight it will be ready to eat.

The straw is tacked with cource thred and needle straw by straw
till it is large enough to include top and bottom 3 qrs of a yd wide

---

* The identity of this person is not known. However, it is worth noticing the
appearance of recipes from 'Lady Hewit' in Martha Bradley's *The British
Housewife*, published in 1756. The modern editor of this work, Gilly Lehmann,
suggests that Lady Hewit was in fact a 17th-century personage, the daughter of
the 1st Earl of Lindsay, wife of Rev. John Hewit (d. 1658), co-conspirator and
associate of Viscount Mordaunt, whose wife was the source of Receipt 225.
There is a further connection to this source via the Onslow family: Evelyn was
on good visiting terms. See the introduction to Martha Bradley for further
details.There is a batch of cheese recipes printed on pp. 88–90 of volume II of
Martha Bradley (to be reprinted in the ongoing Prospect Books facsimile) which
bear tantalizing points of comparison with those found in this MS.
† Meal(e) is an obsolete word for measure (*OED*).
# A variant spelling of the word 'moat', cheese vat (*OED*).   § Weight.
‡ The meaning of this word is inscrutable.
* Lew warm is a variant of lukewarm. 'Lew' itself meant 'warm'. See also 224.
† 'the first' is written above the line.

serves both, in length it may be shorter, two of these will shift the cheese they must be scalded as other fatts.‡

287. A Creame cheese.

Take the creame of 6 bowles and a gallon and halfe of strokings and warme it hot put in a blade of Mace and halfe a nutmeg and 6 spoonfulls of runnet whey it lay it in a wett cloth presse it by degrees[.]

288. A slight way to make a thinn cheese very good.

Take 3 quarts of milk from the Cow set it when it is come lay the curd with a sceming dish in a wett cloth in a shallow fatt or a hoop upon a board lay on all the curd by degrees then cover it and let it sink with its owne weight shift† the cloth 2 or 3 times, the next day lay it on fresh netles shift the netles every day and turne the cheese cover it with netles in 6 dayes it will be fitt to eat. flags are better then netles.*

289. To make Pearle§ Jelly.

Take jelly of calves feet one pint of double refined sugar halfe a pound the juice of 2 lemons the whites of 2 Eggs well beat put these together in a skillet let them boyle a litle while then poure it into a cotton bagg let it run into the glass or cups you would have[.] If it is not cleere the first runing poure it through againe.

290. To make Manger blanc.

take Heartshorne jelly ad to it Almonds beat fine straine it do this till it is as white as you desire it the jelly must be without mixture make it as white as milk sweeten it to yr tast put in a litle Orenge flower

---

‡ i.e. vats.

† i.e. change.

* Subsequent note in MS.

§ Pearl means pellucid.

156

water lay it thinn on a silver plate all over to the brim allmost or fill litle glasses that as you please when it is cold it will cut firme beat the jelly with the Almonds in a Marble morter.

291. To make Flomery.

Let 3 q^{rts} of Oatmell stand 3 dayes in a pot of water before you stirr it then change the water every day 2 Dayes more when you have occasion boyle it 3 q^{rs} of an houre so much as you have need of at a time when it grows thick put in more water.

If you would eat any hot boyle it in the same manner put more water to it let it boyle but a q^r of an houre put in a pint of Renish wine sweeten it to y^r tast and serve it up.

292. An other way to make Flomery.

take a q^r of a peck of the midling sort of flomery oatmell* put to it 3 q^{rts} of water change it twice a day let it lye 2 or 3 dayes the last day poure of some of the cleer take the rest and straine it hard through a strainer then let it stand 2 hours then poure the cleere away take the thick and boyle it leisurly till it grows thinne then it is enough, you may put as much water to the same oatmell and make flomery as good if not better then the first put a litle in when you boyle it.

293. To make Barly Creame.

Take a good quantity of pearle Barley wash it very cleane beat it in a cource cloth a litle and wash it againe put it into a cleane pipkin that is new then boyle it in water a while then poure that away put in fresh water and boyle it as fast as you can till it grows thick then let it run through a strainer then lay a small peece of lemon pill in it and sweeten it with a litle loafe sugar and juice of lemon it makes

---

* John Nott advises the cook to use 'small oatmeal'; Hannah Glasse comments that 'Grotes once cut does better than Oatmeal'.

it pleasant if made in sumer it must be made every day in cold weather it will keepe longer the boyling fast and close covered makes it boyle whitest it is a pleasant messe for a sick person.

294. French fritters.

Take about a q^{rt} of water set it on the fire in a skillet or brasse pan put to it about a q^{r} of a pound of butter some sugar halfe a nutmeg grated when it boyles thicken it with flower till it be a past stir it as fast as you can then take it off set it* by till cold breake in 8 eggs sett it on againe and stir it till as thick as past then take it off when it is allmost coole role it in long roles and cut it in litle peeces as big as nutmegs then strew a litle flower on them and frye them in a pan in hot lard as you do other fritters when they are enough turne them into a cullender to draine then squeeze juice of Orenge and strew sugar on them so serve them up hot.

296. To make an Almond Cake.

Take 6 p[ounds] of the finest flowr drie it in the Oven after bread is drawne next morning rub it through a cource sive blanch 2 p[ounds] of Almonds in cold water beat them with Orenge flower water very fine rub the Almonds into the flower very well then take 3 p[ounds] of the best greene citron cut pretty small and 2 p[ounds] of Eringo root‡ cut small strew these into the flower one Ounce of Nutmegs and mace 3 parts mace† a litle cinamon a litle ginger wash pick and drie 5 pound of Corance lay them on a sive set them before the fire to keepe warme then beat 20 eggs all the whites beat them with a whisk very light straine them take two q^{ts} of the thickest creame put

---

* This word written above the line.

‡ The quantities specified for citron and eringo root both seem very large, by contrast Sir Kenelm Digby's plum cake, made with a peck of flour, required but half a pound of citron.

† i.e. one ounce of nutmeg and mace mixed, in the proportion of three parts mace to one part nutmeg.

it on the fire slice in 4 p[ounds] of the best butter let it stand till
bloud warme a pint and halfe of new ale yest put a glass of sack to
it and the eggs 4 ounces of loafe sugar beat fine strewd in then poure
in the creame and butter on one side the yest and eggs on the other
so melt y^r cake very thinn§ and set it by the fire and at the first rising
put in the corance and let the Oven be ready at the second rising to
put it into the Oven butter the hoop very well it will require somwhat
better then two hours baking Ice it if you please.

297. *To make Royall Marchpane or litle cakes.*

Take one pound of Jordan Almonds blanch them in cold water beat
them very fine put in now and then a litle rose water to keep them
from oyling then take a p[ound] of double refined sugar beat fine and
searced mingle a true halfe of it in the morter with the Almonds then
take it out and make it into cakes then dust sheets of paper with fine
sugar searced and lay them on it set y^r paper of cakes upon a table
then set the baking pan Cover over them with charcoale lighted very
cleere when that side is white and drie set them by to coole awhile
then set the pan on the other side and do as before till they are
enough then take the other part of the sugar and make a candy with
a litle orenge flour or Rose water then take a feather and candy the
cakes they must be candied on both sides set the baking pan to Ice
them as before.†

298. *To make royall Marchpane in round rings.*

Take 2 pound of sweet Almonds and one handfull of bitter ones
blanch them in cold water over night drie them in a cloth beat them
very well then with the whites of three Eggs beat up with Orenge
flower water put to them a p[ound] and halfe of fine sugar sifted set

---

§ 'so melt y^r cake very thinn' is a difficult reading; it is not clear what it means.
† This receipt is interesting about method, particularly its instructions in the use
  of the baking pan, see glossary.

it over a chafing dish with charcoale in a bason or preserving pan stirr it till it is very drie and will work up in to a past then lay it on a cleane board till allmost cold then role it out shape them round let them lye till they are all made then beat 2 or 3 whites of eggs to a froth tosse and wett them all over then tosse them in fine sifted sugar then sift sugar on papers to lay them on set them in an oven that will just couler the paper a q^r of an hour will bake them the oven must be so quick they may rise.*

299. *To make Ginger Bread.*

Take 2 pound of the best flower and 3 quarters of a p[ound] of sweet butter break it small into the flower then put in a pound and halfe of sugar finely beat and two ounces of Ginger beat and sifted the yolks of 4 Eggs the whites of 2, 3 or 4 spoonfulls of sack and as much Ale yest as will make it into a pretty stiffe past if you have no yest it dos as well with eggs only, 7 or 8 halfe the whites will wett the ingredients work into the past a q$^{r.}$ of a p[ound] of greene citron as much candyed Orenge cut in small bitts then role it into long roles or round Cakes as you please just as they are going into the Oven wash them over with a feather dipt in the yolk of an egge beaten, so bake them.

300. *To stew pipins.*

Pare and coare a Dozen pipins very neatly cut them in halfes as quick as you can put to them a pound of double refined sugar a pint of water a few cloves a litle cinamon a litle fresh lemon pill let them boyle pretty quick when the underside is cleere turne them if the syrup grows thick put in 6 spoonfulls of water when they are cleere

---

* Karen Hess, in her learned comments on marchpane, particularly its etymology, observes that the method described in this receipt, where the marchpane is cooked over coals before being glazed and dried or baked, is a French conceit, specified, for instance, by Massialot.

all over lay them in a dish one by one squeeze some juice of lemon straine the Cyrup over the Aples stick some Citron on every peece and bitts of preserved orenge.

301. *To stew pipins to send in with the dessert in halfe sugar.*

Take a dozen of cleere good Kentish pipins pare quarter them and coare them put them into a skillet with as much water as covers them and halfe the weight in fine loafe sugar litle bitts of lemon pill cutt in small* lengths the quantity of halfe a lemon pill in all lett them boyle pretty quick but not to break when they begin to looke cleere put them into a glassed† pan or bason that is deep that the liquor may keep above them cover them close the next day they will look very cleere lay some of them in china or glasse litle basons, and lay the pill on them and liquor to them send them in with the fruit.

302. *To Frye oysters.*

Take Oysters the largest are best drie them in a cloth then flower them on both sides then take 2 or 3 yolks of eggs just break them dip the oysters in let the pan be hot with a bitt of butter fry them browne the sauce may be thick beaten butter or gravy claret with a litle shallot stewed in it then a peece of butter shook in it to thicken the sauce so serve it with the oysters.

303. *To make a Marrow tart.*

Take a q^r of a pound of marrow broken in litle‡ bitts a q^r of a pound of Almonds beat fine with rose water a q^r of a pint of thick creame boyled and cold the yolks of 4 eggs the whites of 2 beat, some citron cut in thinn slices mingle all but the marrow very well some sugar a litle salt a litle spice lay fine past in a patty pan lay this stuffe in

---

* Word written above the line.
† Glazed.
‡ Word written above the line.

it put in the marrow cover it with barrs of past layed crosse the breadth of topeny ruban bake it when neere enough draw it to the ovens mouth Ice it with fine sugar sifted over it and some Orenge flowr or Rose water sprinkled over set it in again till enough. send it in hott.[*]

304. To drie mushroms.

Take mushroms fresh gathered cut in pieces stew them in water and salt then drie them in a Cloth put them in an earthen pot well glased covered close into the oven after bread is drawne repeat this till they are drie then keepe them betweene papers when they are used crumble 3 or 4 into the sauce[.]

305. To Pickle Mushroms.

Peele and put the mushroms in water then put some water over the fire with an onyon and let it boyle put in the mushroms and cover them up close and boyle them quick till they begin to sink then take them out and throw them into cold water and salt and let them lye in the water an houre till they tast of the salt take them out and drie them in a cloth and make a pickle with white wine and vinegar and all sorts of spice a little lemon pill a bay leafe do not boyle it but put the mushroms in [in]† a wide mouthed glasse keepe them covered for use.

306. A pickle for mushrooms.

A quart of the best wine vinegar a quart of white wine Cloves Mace Nuttmegs bruised boyle all well together till halfe a pint of the liquor is consumed let it stand till quite cold then poure it on the Mushroms leave none of the spice in that was boyled in the liquor but put in fresh quartering the Nutmeg a little lemon pill some white pepper a whole raw Onyon when the Onyon begins to perish take it out[.]

---

* This last instruction a subsequent note added in the MS.

† Repetition in MS.

307. To pickle Capers.

Gather the caper buds before they are quite blowne lay them in the shade 3 or 4 hours put them in a vessell poure vinegar on them cover the vessell with a board so let them stand 9 dayes then take them out and presse them gently and put them in fresh vinegar. Let them stand as long as before repeat it a third time then barrell them up with vinegar and a litle salt.

308. To Pickle Wallnuts.

Take wallnuts before they grow hard salt and boyle them when the water coulers shift them do so 3 times scuming them clean when they are litle soft wipe them and when cold put them in a wide mouthed glasse or glazed pot laying some dill to cover the bottom then lay a row of the nuts on them strew a handfull of salt then Dill so more nuts salt and dill till the pot is 3 q^{rs} full then put in ginger cloves whole mace and peper some garlick then fill it up with the best white wine vinegar and Mustard stop it close and let it stand two or 3 months this makes them as good if not better then Mango being scraped into sauce thickens it[.]§

309. To dose hams with hott salt.

Cutt the legs of pork like Westphalia hams set (as much white salt as you think will cover so many hams as you intend to salt) on the fire that it may be very hott and dry put two ounces of piter salt† beaten very fine to every legge mingled with the white salt the salt must be layd on as hott as possible and as close as can be that no ayre come neere the hams which if large may ly in salt 15 dayes the small ones tenn day will suffice 3 weeks or a month will drie them if the fire is constant tho small it is better to rub the saltpeter on first

§ Compare this receipt with that in *Acetaria*.

† Saltpetre. White salt is rock salt or salt obtained by boiling rather than natural evaporation.

cold on the hams then the hott salt presently after breake the knucle bone and put salt in they are best don in cold weather and salted as soone as cut out.

310. To salt Bacon my Lady Claytons‡ way.

Take a gallon of water a pound of cource sugar mixed wash the hams or Bacon rubing it with this an houre then rub it with halfe bay salt and halfe white very well then let it lye in the salt 2 Dayes and one night then shake of the salt and take as much sall prunella as will lye on two five shilling peeces mixed with as much common white salt which is enough for an ordinary sized Gamon so proportionably for a flitch let them ly in some leaden trough that will hold brine Turne the under side upermost everie day be sure to rub the knucles and places that are apt to lye drie do thus 7 or 8 dayes then hang it up to smoake the ribbs will be salt enough in 6 dayes.

The best way to smoke them is in a close loft with saw dust which will do in 4 dayes or at most in a weeke in a Chimney with wood smoake it requires a longer time.

311. To stew a Breast of Veale in Ragout.

Take a small white fat Midle sized breast of Veale, roast 3 q^{rs} scure it to the spit take it off lay it in a stew pan that fitts put to it a pint of strong broath some claret or white wine some gravy of alltogether enough to cover it put in whole piper a blade or two of mace a bunch

---

‡ Most probably Lady Martha (c.1643–1705), daughter of Perient Trott, wife of Sir Robert Clayton (1629–1707), scrivenor, politician and Lord Mayor of London. They were neighbours of the Evelyns at Bletchingley and Marden in Surrey. The first was sold to him through the agency of Evelyn to settle Lord Peterborough's debts, the second was bought from the estate of Sir John Evelyn, JE's cousin. On visiting Marden in 1677, Evelyn commented that Lady Clayton was 'very curious in distillery'. He was impressed by the Claytons' planting and orchards. On dining at the Guildhall at the Lord Mayor's banquet in 1679 he observed that Clayton had married 'a free-hearted woman, who became his hospitable disposition.'

of sweet herbs a peece of Onyon a litle salt stew it till it is very tender, then add Balls of veale pistache nuts chestnuts roasted and peeled parboyle the sweetbread and [and]* cut it in pretty broad slices season it a litle dip it in the yolks of Eggs and frye it, put some of the farced meat such as the balls into litle pasties of puffe past frye them Clarie leaves fryed in Egge do well Hartichoke botoms cut in quarters do well stewed with the veale allso some coxcombs that are first scalded and peeled, when all is ready lay the veale in the dish, slip out some of the long bones, lay the od[d]† things round and upon the veale the fryed sweetbreads and Clary upermost, the pasties to garnish the dish with fryed parsly betweene, then take the onyon spice and herbs out of the sauce and shake in a good peece of butter with it thicken it with yolks of Eggs and poure it into the dish to the meat.

To make gravy Take some steaks of leane beef as many as will lye on the bottom of the frying pan slash them with a knife strew salt in them put to them about a quart of water a piece of an onion some whole Peper and a bundle of sweet herbs so set the frying pan over the fire to stew till the meat is hard then take that gravy and use in y^r stewed veale.

312. An Aple tart the Queene Mothers‡ way.

Take a large lemon cut off the paring quick that not the least speck of white remains on the lemon cut it in qrs pick out every seed and cut the quarters in slices as thinne as paper set them by then pare off the pill of a Civill oringe so thinn it may be yellow on both sides, shred it as small as pens heads then make the past thus break 3 Eggs into a qt of fine flower with a litle water 3 q^rs of a p[ound] of fresh

---

* Repeated in the MS.
† Supplied.
‡ Presumably Queen Henrietta Maria.

Butter handle the past as litle as possible when you have roled all the butter in role the past out as thin as you think fitt cover the patty pan which must be well flowred before have a pound of fine loafe sugar beat ready to go through the sive then pare a Dozen of faire good kentish pipins the cours scraped out pare them neatly and drie them quick and then strow Orenge pill on the bottom then lay a row of the sliced pipin some slices of the lemon on them sift sugar over them then more Aples and lemon some Orenge pill and sugar soi do till all are in last of all sugar at top then cover it with past bake it in a quick Oven when you take it out cut of the lid and cut it in 4 q^{rs} to lay round the tart with in side and puffs round the brim of the dish which you may make of the past that is left cut them in fashion you like role the past pretty thick that they may rise the higher lay them on papers flowred and baked with the tart[.]

get some jelly of pipins to cover the tart with when it comes out of the Oven with juice of Orenge in it put it on warme it is best to make this tart in the morning that it may be just cold when to be eat but it may be good if made over night[.]

313. Another way to stew a breast of Veale en Ragout.

Season a fine small white breast of Veale with mace nutmeg salt and pepper a few sweet herbs fasten it with scures[*] to the spitt bast it well and halfe roast it then put a pint of white wine as much gravy to the meat which must be layed in a stew pan that is long and fitt the meat some strong broath allso alltogether enough to cover the meat then put in a pallet of beef parboyled [and boyled tender][†] cut in slices fryed browne some coxcombs lambstone a sweetbread or two all scalded sliced and fryed browne halfe a pint of mushroms some balls of farced meat let all these stew together if in season you may

---

* Skewers.

† This comment added subsequently; note the entry in the glossary relating to 'parboiled'.

put in greene goosberies hartichoke bottoms halfe boyled first or greene grapes som yolks of hard Eggs lemon cut in dice add to the sauce two anchoves if you love it a q^r of a pound of sweet butter shake all these together then set the dish to keep warme lay the meat in then the odd things upon and round it you may have tenne or twelve collets* of mutton ready broyled seasoned and breaded to lay round the dish poure the sauce on as hot as you can over the meat so send it in.

314. To make cotlets of veale the french way.

Take the ribs of a litle white neck of Veale hack them very well and season them with nutmeg salt and pepper then halfe broyle them then beat 2 or 3 Eggs and some grated bread lay it thinne over the meat then frye them a litle for the sauce take a pint of strong gravy boyled with two Anchovis a litle samphier the juice of an orenge frye some slices of Bacon lay them on the bottom of y^r dish then lay the collets* on them, then some fryed Oysters and sassages, lay on the top more slices of bacon fryed and fryed parsly then put in the sauce let all things be ready together that the cotlets may be eat hott.

315. To dresse Rabets.

Boyle a couple of Rabets with a large handfull of parsly and two great onions in the belly of each when they are boyled pull them in small peeces and season them with salt then desolve two Anchovies in six spoonfulls of Claret wine and 4 of vinegar and put it to the Rabets the onyon and parsly taken out of the rabets must be choped very small together and put other to them set all on the fire so stew till the sauce is soaked up then put 3 q^{rs} of a pound of butter in shake all well and send it in hott to the table.

---

* The spelling 'collets' is not a variant recorded in *OED* for 'cotlets' but that is what is plainly meant, if not written.

316. To Coller Beefe my L. Glandvilles way.†

Take 6 penny worth of salt peter and a litle bay salt and rub the beefe all over role it up and let it lye 24 hours Make a brine with bay salt and water strong enough to bear an Egge put the beefe in which must be a piece of thinne flanc let it ly in 9 dayes then take it out hang it up awhile till it is well drained, take off the loose skins and white leathers‡ then shred parsly sweet Marjoram thime winter savory enough to strew it all over allso Nutmeg mace cloves and a litle pepper beat role it up hard and bind it about with tape like a coller of brawne put it into an earthen glazed pot cover it with spring water and put a litle whole spice into the water, past it over with cource dough put it into the Oven with houshold bread and let it stand all night when you draw it out of the Oven the next morning take it out of the pot as hott as you can without breaking it, role it in a cource cloth then tye the tapes harder that were loosened in the baking role it againe so let it remaine till cold.

317. To pot pidgeons.

Pull† yᵉ pidgeons and take out the craws but do not draw them then bone them whole beginning at the neck loose the sinews about the leggs and wings with a small knife and draw out the bones then put them into spring water 2 hours then take them out and draine them well and drie every single pidgeon in a cloth then season them with white peper cloves mace beat nuttmeg grated puting some into everyone and rubing the outsides so let them lye together all night next morning do the like with salt which if don over night with the

---

† i.e., 'my L[ady] Glandville's way'. Mary Evelyn's great-aunt was Winifred (Bourchier), wife of Sir John Glanville (1586–1660), speaker of the Short Parliament. The Diary records a visit to his country seat at Broad Hinton in Wiltshire in 1654. They returned the call to Sayes Court in later years.

‡ White can be the flank of an ox (butchery); leather was the outer skin (*OED*).

† Pluck (obs. or dialect, *OED*).

spice would make them look red so stuffe every pidgeon with another the least and worst rump to neck and breast to back that fat and leane be mixed* 3 or 4 hours after sett on a quantity of butter in a tinned saucepan or stewpan when it boyles and is scumed put in as many pidgeons as it will hold conveniently and let them boyle but gently keeping them scumed and turning pretty often till they are enough then take them up draning the gravy from them and place them in the pot and set more a boyling to do to many together does but wast the butter a pretty large pott full will require to be done at 3 times this done either presently or next morning take some of the butter they were boyled in clear it from the gravy and melt with more and clarifie it and fill up the pot or potts in litle ones they do best because they will not keepe long when cutt.

318. To stew a Turky and chicken the french way.

Take a turky of a midle size take out the breast bone take 4 or 6 chicken of a midle size fill their bellies with farce meat of veale and beefe suet shred very fine seasoned with mace nutmeg pepper and salt work it up with 3 or 4 yolks of raw Eggs, then set them in scallding water you may lard the breast of the Turky, then flowr and frye them pretty browne then have strong broath and stew them leisurly in it, then get a strong soupe with gravy shallot a blade of mace some sweet breads and lamb stones first scalded peeled cutt in slices and fryed a litle, bottoms of hartichokes do well halfe boyled first, 6 or 8 hard yolks of Eggs, some fryed slices of bacon dipped in raw Eggs and parsly shred, a q^{rt} of gravy will suffice to stew these things in, when ready stirr in halfe a pound of butter the juice of an

---

* Although the syntax appears inscrutable, it makes sense. If comparison is made to other recipes, it was evidently considered important that the flesh should be mixed with adequate fat. Hence Charles Carter (*The Complete Practical Cook*, 1730) advises that when you stove pigeons for potting some are larded, others are left plain.

orenge, so shake all together then place the Turky in the midle the chickens round and all the other things betweene and about [the other things betweene and about]‡ the Turky and Chickens lay some on the breast serve it up hott with the sauce.

319. To make a Bisk of Carps.

Take twelve male Carps draw them cut of their heads take out their toungs and melts take the flesh from the bones of the Carps then take 50 oysters some midling bacon some sweet herbs some grated bread, the yolks of 10 hard Eggs hash all these together season it with Nuttmegs cloves and salt to this add the yolks of five raw Eggs, and make it pretty stiffe in the fashion of roles or balls, stew them in a deep stew pan with a q^t of oysters 2 Anchovis the melts and heads of the Carps a pound of fresh butter some of the oyster liquor the juice of one or two lemons some white wine some gravy of veale or mutton one whole onyon let them all stew upon a soft fire, then have in a readinesse a great male Carp very well scaled and drawne lay it in white wine with 3 Anchovis stew it with† lemon pill large Mace and Onyon when you dresse up y^r dish lay the great carp in the midle range the 12 heads about it then the balls the melts and toungs with the oysters thicken y^r sauce with 3 yolks of Eggs the juice of two orenges serve it up hott[.]

320. To make a Carpe potage.

Take two Carps strip them then take all the fleshy part of the Carps and hash it very small then stew it in a litle butter with some crums of bread then hash it againe then cut the bones of the carps cut a litle onyon and crusts of bread and frye it with [herbs]* a litle bunch of sweet herbs then take out some of the bones and put liquor of peas

---

‡ The phrase in square brackets was reapeated in error in the MS.
† This word is written above the line.
* Superfluous.

to it let all boyle 2 or 3 hours then beat the bones that are taken out in a Morter then frye them in browne butter and flowr then put some of y^r liquor to it and let it boyle a litle then pour it through a strainer and put the hash to it then soake bread with some of the liquor that is cleere and when it is soaked put the hash in it and serve it up salt must not be omitted nor a litle spice in the stewing.

321. To make Crawfish Potage.[†]

Take two small carps that are Melters scale them then open them and take out the Melts save them then wash out the bloud with Claret wine save that, then take off their skinns as whole as you can lay them by, then take the flesh cleane off from the bones then boyle the heads and bones in 4 quarts of spring water with a litle salt a whole Onyon a few cloves when it is well boyled straine it and keepe the broath for the Crawfish, then take 4 dozen of crawfish boyle them in water and salt some vinegar when they are boyled pick the tayls and claws frye them in sweet butter save a dozen of the Body shells whole to garnish with then take the bodyes of the rest and shelle and beat them in a stone Morter with a dozen of hard yolks of eggs and the crum of a manchet a litle beaten pepper ginger nutmeg and salt then put the broath of the carps to it and let all soake on the fire then straine it and keepe it for use, then mince halfe the fish of the carps with a litle greene parsly some nutmeg pepper and grated bread sweet herbs shred and sweet butter, work it up alltogether and stuffe the skins of the Carps with some of this farce, then stuffe the dozen shells that were saved for garnish with the same then parboyle the other halfe of the fish and mince it as you do a hash then put in y^r

---

† The distinction between the bisk and the potage, in this instance, would appear to be that the first was a stew with liquor and solids, while the second was closer to an emulsified soup thickened with flour. The bisk begins in a similar vein to Robert May's receipt for the same dish which in turn was a version of that found in *The Compleat Cook*. When John Nott repeated it in his invaluable *Dictionary*, he entitled it 'A Bisk or Pottage...'.

wine and bloud and a litle butter with a shallot set them over the embers to stew a litle then put in the farce meats which are in the shells and the carp in the skinns into a pan, with a litle butter let them stew covered close, then take the crusts of two french roles or loaves, toast them very browne, and break them into the bottome of the dish then put in y^r broath when the bread is wetted and well soaked up, with the crawfish broath, then lay on the tayles and fee[t]* which were fryed, strew them all over the dish, then the hash which is stewd in the wine and bloud, then place that in the shells and skinns allso the Melts then scatter the spawne all over, the dish must be kept warme over the fire all the time it is filling.

322. *A Plum Cake (Mrs E Packer).*†

Take 4 pound of flowr well dryed two pound of butter a qrt of good creame, halfe a pound of loafe sugar beat, a pint of good Ale yest 14 or 16 Eggs leaving out halfe the whites six pound of Corrance well washed picked and dried, halfe an ounce of mace, of Cinnamon and Nutmeg each a q^r of an Ounce, a few cloves as much salt as may ly upon a shilling a q^r or halfe a pint of sack the yest must be neither bitter nor thin nor with the drink but indifferent thick and light, straine it through a sive and put some of the sack to it and set it neere the fire to grow warm and work up, beat the sugar salt and spice very fine put them together and mingle them with the flower after you have rubbed in a pound of the butter, then set the creame over the fire and let it boyle then put in the other pound of butter cutt in bitts take off the creame stirr and ladle it up thick as for sauce, so set it by to be but bloud warme when you use it, a litle Rose water dos well in the creame keepe out a litle of the creame and of the sacke

---

* The 't' is supplied, presumably what is meant is the claws.
† This may be a member of the Packer family, of Groombridge, Kent., although the reading is doubtful. The wife of Evelyn's 'old and worthy friend' Philip Packer, deputy-surveyor of the King's Works, was called Isabel.

least it should make the cake too thinn or should want at last then
warme it and put in, beat the Eggs and straine them then lay the
flowr up high in the midle with a trench round poure in the Eggs
creame and yest severally at 3 sides and by degrees and stirr it round
with a wooden spatula or slice till all is wett and beat it up very light,
strewing in the corrance when it is all wett, and set it before the fire
for halfe an houre or 3 q^{rs} till it rises light, covering it with a sheet
of paper dried hott at the fire, and turne the dish about somtimes, that
it may take heat and rise all alike, have the hoop ready buttered with
2 or 3 papers at the bottom which will help to keep the bottom of the
cake from burning, when the Oven is ready beat up the cake againe
and put it into the hoop it must be wett as it were a puding or fine
batter, you may add Citron or Orenge or both, it will require two
hours baking and the oven stoped after the scorching is over, and a
sheet or two of paper‡ as you see occasion dried and layed on the top
of the cake to keepe it from too much Coloring, if you tye packthreds
across the top of the hoop to fasten the bottom papers remember to
cutt them when it is in the oven, you must tye them and fitt the hoop
ready for the cake and to poure in the batter between the packthreds
dont tye the hoop to wide to make the cake too flatt and thinne, ice
it as you do other cakes

323-331. [Receipts for drinks, omitted.]

332. To make Naples biscuit.

Take 6 or 7 Eggs yolks and whites the treads being taken away beat
the Eggs a q^r of an hour then put to them a pound of loafe sugar beat
and sifted beat all a q^r of an houre more then take 3 q^{rs} of a pound
of fine flowr and beat it a q^r of an houre then disolve a litle musk in
some rose water warme a graine is enough add that to the batter then

---

‡ 'of paper' is written above the line.

butter the coffins and fill them then bake them in an oven as hot as for manchet.

333. To make Shrewsbery cakes.

Take 2 p[ounds] of flowr one p[ound] of butter 3 q^{rs} of a p[ound] of sugar beat and sifted 4 eggs two Races of ginger grated and searced rub the butter into the flowr then put in the sugar and spice then wett it with the Eggs when it is in a past role the Cakes of an indifferent thickness with as litle flower as you can cut them round with a glasse prick them with the great teeth of a comb that is new and kept for that use lay them on papers a litle floured bake them in an oven that is not to hott.

334. An other way for Shrewsberie Cakes.

Take one pound of flowr well dried one pound of butter halfe a pound of sugar beat and sifted 4 yolks of Eggs beat the Eggs and sugar together then mix in the butter strew in the flowr by degrees make it into a past role it of a reasonable thicknesse cut the cakes of what size you like with the foot of a glasse or other convenient thing if you love coriander seeds you may put some in bake them let the oven not be too hott.

335. To pickle Cowcumbers like Mango.

Take great Cowcumbers that are of the size of Mangoes and look greene open them on the sides take out the seeds and put into them a litle clove of garlicke, then put them into an earthen vessel with as much white wine vinegar whole pepper cloves mace as will cover them boyle in the vinegar the spice but put salt into it when it is off the fire, as much as makes it a gentle brine, then poure it boyling hot upon the Cowcumbers cover them close till the next day then put the Cowcumber with a litle dill and the pickle into a large skillet or pot boyle them a boyle or two, then put them into an earthen pot againe and cover them close when they are cold put in a large spoonfull of beat mustard seed, keepe them from the ayre, when you take them out do it with a spoon not with y^r fingers.[†]

336. To Dresse Whitings.

Take whitings fresh caught chop off their heads flay them scotch them in severall gashes with a knife strew salt on them lay them in an earthen dish to draine the water from them fry them in buter being flowred melted butter for the sauce this way of dressing them makes them far exceed soles and eat admirably well.

337 To dresse a pike. My Ld St Albans way.[*]

Take a large male pike cutt in 8 peeces take 3 pints of white wine 3 pints of white wine vinegar more or lesse of both so there be enough to cover the fish 6 onyons 2 heads of garlick cut in bitts a bundle of sweet herbs thime Marjoram a little Mint Rosmary parsly all tyed up with a litle thred put allso a lemon cut in slices 2 or 3 handfulls of salt this liquor must boyle on a quick fire before the pike goes in then let it boyle covered when enough take it up and draine it well then have the dish ready rub the bottom with garlick.

For the sauce disolve 4 or 6 Anchovies in a litle wine straine it then put to some of it some butter to melt by degrees about 2 p[ounds] beat it up thick, in the melting put in by degrees 2 spoonfulls of the liquor the pike was boyled in cut a lemon in bitts without the rind mingle it with the sauce then place the pike cover

---

[†] Compare this to Receipt 262, above.

[*] Presumably Henry Jermyn (d. 1684), first Earl of St Albans, Lord Chamberlain. Evelyn describes him memorably towards the end of a long life, 'He eate and drank with extraordinary appetite' (Diary, 18 September 1683). Sir Kenelm Digby included a receipt for 'cresme fouettee' from Lord St Albans. In 1666, Evelyn wrote to his wife that none greeted him at court 'with more ceremony, compliment and wonderful expressions of kindness, than my Lord of St. Albans who is wont (you know) to overlook all the world.' (Hiscock, p. 64.)

it with the sauce some sippets if you please garnish with Barberies lemon and tuffts of horse Radish scraped.

338. The Lady Evelyns† way to make white Meath.

Take 6 gallons of water boyle it halfe an houre, then let it stand till cold then put so much hony as will make it bear an Egge then set in the ketle againe, let it boyle as fast as it can, in the boyling put in 10 eggs well beat shells and all, throw into it a handfull of rosmary tops, and when it has boyled a while scum it very cleer then slice 2 Ounces of ginger into an earthen stand and poure the liquor to it, set it to work with yest spread on both sides of a toast well baked put it into a vessell stop it up, if fine in a fortnights time botle it, otherwise stay longer, drink of it 3 weeks after.

339. To make goosberie wine fr Chris: wren.*

Take goosberies droping ripe next to rottenesse squeeze them to mash thick as mustard let it work and be well scumed, tun up the cleere and it will ferment again being kept 2 yeare it is an excellent wine.

340. To make a carraway puding to bake L. Gland:†

Take 3 pints and halfe of new Milk and 3 q^{rs} of a pound of butter and set them on the fire together, then take a pint and 3 q^{rs} of flower and wett it with 5 eggs leaving out 3 whites and so make it with cold milk as thin as batter then sweeten to y^r tast add some nuttmeg grated and a handfull of carrawayes stirred in it, then take the milk

---

† There are several Lady Evelyns who might be referred to here, but perhaps the most likely is Thomasine, née Heynes, wife of Sir John Evelyn of Godstone (1591–1664), JE's first cousin. Alternatively, his son, who died in 1671, was married firstly to Mary, née Farmer. She died in 1663.

* Sir Christopher Wren (1632–1723), architect.

† See Receipt 316 for presumably the same 'L[ady] Gland[ville]'.

off which is boyling on the fire and straine it all together into y^r dish and put a q^r of a pound of butter in small bitts so bake it in a quick oven.

341.   Past for pattypan tarts.

Take to a pound and quarter of flowr 2 ounces of sugar beaten one egg and halfe a pound of butter work the butter into the flower then beat the Egge with the sugar and as much water as will wett it into a pretty light past sheet the patty pans lay in the fruit with as much sugar as you think convenient close them and melt butter and water indifferent thick wash them over and searce fine sugar on them bake them halfe an hour[.]

342.   To make cold water past.

Take 2 pound of flowr a pound of butter rub a q^r of a pound of the butter into the flower take the yolks of two Eggs beat them put as much water as will mix the flower into a light past then put in the other 3 quarters of a pound of butter at three times be sure to role it allwayes one way.

343.   To make french Bread.

Take a gallon of flowr take 3 whites of Eggs beat them well and mix them with a pint of good Ale yest, take some new milk and a litle water set it over the fire put in a q^r of a pound of butter make it hott enough to melt it, mix it with the Eggs and yest, then mix up the bread as slight* as for a cake let it rise a q^r of an houre lay the loaves upon flowred paper what bignesse you please the oven must be well heat an hour bakes them.

---

* 'Slight' is used here in its meaning of smooth.

John Evelyn's monogram, taken from the title page of *Sculptura*.

Glossary

ALE PINT: see WEIGHTS AND MEASURES.

ALLUM, ALUM: called by Evelyn 'roch-allum' in *Acetaria*, is an astringent salt, a double sulphate of aluminium and potassium, used in pickling and bread baking, as well as fabric dying (Hess).

AMBERGRECE, AMBERGREASE, AM. GREEC, AMBREGREECE, AMBERGRICE, AMBER: ambergris. The *Encyclopaedia Britannica*, 11th edition, describes it as a 'biliary concretion in the intestines' of the sperm whale, found either floating in the sea, or in the abdomens or intestinal tracts of dead whales. It is a 'solid, fatty, inflammable substance of a dull grey or blackish colour, the shades being variegated like marble, possessing a peculiar sweet, earthy odour.' It was much used in cookery, but is now restricted to perfumery. The glossary to Joan Cromwell's cookery book describes the perfume of ambergris as 'the blending of new-mown hay with the scent of violets.'

AÑA: of each alike. (See WEIGHTS AND MEASURES.)

ANGELOTS: round Norman cheeses named after the coin called the angelot (picturing St Michael slaying the dragon) minted in Paris during the English occupation by Henry VI, and later, by King Louis XI of France. The *OED* cites a definition in Cotgrave's English-French dictionary of 1611. Patrick Rance (*The French Cheese Book*) gives examples of cheeses beyond the Norman border that took the name. In fact, the name predates Henry VI, and may have had nothing to do with the coin, but all with the Pays d'Auge, whence originated Camembert. The earliest mention of angelot, Rance confirms, is in the *Roman de la Rose* in the early 13th century. Compare the recipe here with that in *The Compleat Cook*.

APPLES: there were several apple varieties current, and mention is made of some of them in the text. The most convenient summary of varieties is in the glossary to Hannah Glasse.

   CODLINS: small green apples that were suitable for coddling (gently boiling). However, Karen Hess makes clear that the etymology of the two words is different. The apple word derived from a Middle English term meaning 'hard'; the cookery descriptor came from the Norman French *caudeler*, to heat gently – the same root, she points out, as the word 'caudle', and coddle as in coddled eggs.

PEARMAINS: a tall five-faceted, dual-purpose apple.

PIPPINS: sweet apples, that were raised from imported European stock. The skin was usually flecked with gold. Receipt 301 specifies Kentish pippins. Davidson, in the glossary to Hannah Glasse, notes that the Red Kentish Pippin was first mentioned by the botanist John Ray in 1665.

ASHENKEY: ash key, the seed of the ash, usually pickled, as in Receipt 131.

BAKING PAN: Receipt 297 contains several references to the use of a baking pan to make marchpane. It advises that the sheets of marchpane should be laid on a table and a baking pan cover put over them, 'with charcoale lighted very clear'. Kenelm Digby records different details, but points up the function of the baking pan: 'You must have a pan like a tourtiere, made to contain coals on the top, that is flat, with edges round about to hold in the coals, which set over the Cakes, with fire upon it. Let this remain upon the Cakes, till you conceive, it hath dryed them sufficiently for once; ...pull the Papers [on which the marchpane was laid] ...and turn them upon new Papers...remove the pan...to dry their other side.' The baking pan, therefore, was like a Roman *clibanus*, a vessel that could have coals heaped on all sides, and on the top, in the hearth to replicate the function of an oven – like the pot ovens used in western districts of the British Isles. Most contemporary recipes for marchpane include reference to the baking pan, though not all of them specify how it should be used. For example, *A Queens Delight* states that the marchpane should be baked 'in an Oven, or in a Baking-pan'. There is a mention in Sir Hugh Plat's *Delightes for Ladies* of an instrument he calls a 'campaign stove' which must have been akin.

BARLEY, FRENCH: a form of pearl or pot barley. *OED* quotes the *Family Herbal* of 1789 which defines French barley as being skinned, with the ends ground off. Pearl barley is a further refinement of the grain. Elinor Fettiplace describes in her receipts the preparation of French barley by soaking barley corn, beating it with a beetle in a sack, then rubbing, winnowing and wetting it again before drying the grains in the oven.

BASEL: (?) basil. Although this word occurs in Receipt 191 (To pickle salmon), it is not certain it is an accurate transcription, nor may it ever have been the intended meaning. It is added above the line, apparently qualifying the word 'spices' and it seems an unexpected element in the recipe. No other occurrence of the herb exists in the manuscript.

BASSE: bass, bast, a string or tape of straw or bark, specifically of lime or linden, used here to bind up a collar of bacon (Receipt 20). The word bast is found today in stitchery, and in raffia-work.

BATLDORE: battledore. One used battledores to smash shuttlecocks over the net. In other words, the battledore was a paddle-like instrument, used primarily in the laundry, to beat things with. Receipt 210, for wafers, in which this implement figures is interestingly detailed in matters of equipment and method.

BEAT: stamp (q.v.) or grind, e.g. 'beat mustard seed'.

BEATILLO: derived from the French *béatilles*, which word denotes, according to *Larousse Gastronomique* (1938 edn.), small articles such as cockscombs, chicken kidneys, and lambs' sweetbreads that are used as fillings for *vol-au-vents*, *tourtes* and *bouchées*. Robert May calls his beatillo pie batalia.

BEET, BEETE: *Beta vulgaris*, the leaf beet (red, white or black), not the root, is often meant when, as in Receipt 40, Evelyn suggests adding beetes along with potherbs. White beets are suggested in Receipts 182 and 184. These are what we call Swiss Chard (see *Acetaria*).

BETONY: *Stachys officinalis*.

BISK: bisque. Note Receipts 319–21 for bisks and potages.

BLOODING: a black or blood pudding; cf. 'livering': a liver pudding.

BRAWN, BRAWNE: flesh, suitable for roasting, usually the better bits, a citation in *OED* uses the word to distinguish the breast of fowl from its leg. Evelyn refers to the 'brawne of an hen' in his Receipt 16 for mangar blanch, echoing countless medieval recipes for similar dishes which likewise specify brawn of birds. Its restriction to meat from a pig was not then universal.

BREAD: there were several sorts of bread current at the period, some of which are referred to below:

FRENCH BREAD: yeasted bread made with a dough enriched with milk and eggs. In Receipt 183 is a reference to both white and brown French bread. Receipt 273 states that if no French bread is available, a smaller quantity of good white bread should be substituted.

FRENCH ROULE: presumably a small round loaf of 'French' bread.

HOUSEHOLD BREAD: the standard bread, made from coarser flour than manchet, but usually with some bran removed. Referred to in Receipt 316.

MANCHET: yeasted bread made from the whitest flour. Baked in a slightly cooler oven than household bread.

PENNY LOAF: a loaf which could be bought for a penny – which of course varied with the price of wheat, and the grade of flour, and so forth. Karen Hess expands on the theme, with the advice of Elizabeth David (see pp. 109-110 of *Martha Washington's Booke of Cookery*), with the suggestion that a penny loaf of white flour might have weighed between 12 and 16 ounces, and a penny roll or manchet of the very finest flour might have been half that size. The problem is that a size was understood, irrespective of the day-to-day variation in price.

TWOPENNY (TOPENY) LOAF: cost twice as much and was twice as large.

BROOKLIME, BROOK LYME: *Veronica beccabunga*.

BROOME BUDS: buds of the broom, usually pickled, were used in place of capers.

CANTIMPLORA: the word is Italian, in Spanish it is *cantinplora*. In the text, and the appended footnote, is information about these, but this letter from the late Elizabeth David to the present editor throws more light on their use and characteristics. 'I am amused,' she wrote, 'to hear that Evelyn was interested in these devices. A cantimplora was – still is – a glass vessel with a big belly and a long neck. Half up the body of the vessel is a deep pocket in which ice or snow is inserted, thereby indirectly cooling the wine in the vessel without diluting or in any way damaging it.

'The cantimplora in Evelyn's drawing is lying on its side, and if one didn't already know what it's supposed to be it would be quite a puzzle. (I happen to own one from the days when I used to go from time to time to Malta, where these vessels were in common use.) Round about the 1660s, Tuscan nomenclature changed, and a cantimplora became the term applied to an ice bucket which was then a pretty new idea. I didn't know that the cork ice bucket was also called a cantimplora.'

CARDOON: see THISTLE.

CHAFING DISH: a portable brazier holding charcoal, set on a metal stand, that acted as a stove away from the heat of the main kitchen fire. 'A portable grate for coals' (Johnson's *Dictionary*).

CHALDERON, CHATHERN: chawdron, entrails.

CHESFAT: cheese vat, the mould in which the curds are pressed to make cheese.

CHINE: 'the whole or part of the backbone of an animal, with the adjoining flesh' (*SOED*).

CITTRON, citron: *Citrus medica*, see Davidson, *Fruit*, for a discussion of its virtues. It was usually employed, for instance in Receipt 140, for its peel. It is sometimes distinguished as 'green citron'.

CIV: sieve.

CLARRETT, CLARRET, CLARET, WINE: claret. Although the usage that invariably linked claret to the wines of Bordeaux was current from about the year 1600 (*OED*), the earlier meaning, which distinguished wines of a claret colour (orange or light red, i.e. the French *clairet*) from white or fully red wines, was still found. See, for instance, the use in Receipt 129 where the maker of cherry wine is to add 'white or clarrett wine into each bottle'. Hess has a useful discussion of this point.

CLARY, CLARIE: clary, *Salvia sclarea*. Clary leaf fritters are specified in Receipt 311. Clary was otherwise used medicinally.

CLODDES: clots, or lumps.

CLOVE JULY FLOWER, JULYFLOWER: clove-gillyflower (*Dianthus caryophyllus*) or clove-scented pinks.

COALS: in most cases where this word is used, the meaning is charcoal – as might be employed in a chafing dish. There are references to wood fires, for instance in Receipt 151, where 'it must be very quick'.

COCK TREADINGS, TREADS: opaque speck on the yolk of a fertilised egg, usually removed by straining.

COFFINS: moulds or cases of raised hot-water paste, used as containers for any number of dishes, from meat pies to cheesecakes. Where they were made of coarse pastry, it is not inevitable that they would have been eaten. They were more a way of getting food through the baking process that anything else. In Receipt 154 are instructions for blind-baking a coffin for cheesecake. The pastry is pricked all over and filled with bran, rather than our current favourite of beans or ceramic beans. Receipt 244 says that you should butter your coffins before filling them with Naples biscuit mixture. In this instance, the word is used to describe a baking tin, rather than pastry case.

COLIANDER: coriander.

COLLAR: a collar of beef, or any other meat, or fish, was a boned and rolled joint, bound with tapes, threads or cloths, that was usually pickled or brined before boiling.

COLLOPS: thin slices of meat. In Receipt 232[bis], the collops are 'hacked' which usually means cut into smaller pieces. It almost seems as if the *escalopes* (note the phonetic, perhaps even philological, connection between the two words) have been cut further to become *scaloppini*. Compare with Hess's remarks on this word. Collops are still current usage in Scotland.

COLUMBINE, COLLOMBINE LEAVES: from *Aquilegia vulgaris*, are used in Receipt 184, although normally restricted to medicinal receipts.

COMFITT, COMFIT: sugar-coated grains, seeds, or small aromatic substances. Hence amber comfits in Receipt 61 were grains of ambergris coated in hard sugar. The most common were caraway comfits. Aniseed balls are their modern descendants.

CORINTHS: currants, also called raisins of Corinth.

CORN: green corn was used in tansies as a colouring agent.

COURSE: see SERVICE.

CUE: the use of this word in Receipt 57 is not certain. In his instructions for mustard-making in *Acetaria*, Evelyn advises the cook to sieve (searce) through tiffany (fine silk). It is possible that the word is used here in the manuscript to denote a vessel, perhaps an abbreviation of cucurbit, which was a gourd-shaped glass used in distillation, the lower part of an alembic. The *OED* records Evelyn's recommendation in *Kalendarium Hortense* (1664) of the 'new-invented cucurbit-glass' as a trap to catch insects in the garden.

CURRANS, CORRANCE: currants.

DIAPER NAPKIN: referred to in Receipt 99, is a linen napkin woven with a characteristic diamond pattern.

DORCASSE SEED: daucus seed, i.e. the seed of *Daucus carota*, the wild carrot. John Nott has a recipe for 'Another Purging Ale' which includes a vast number of bitter and strong agents, including 'Daucus-Seeds'. Gerard thought them a remedy for falling-sickness (Grigson, *The Englishman's Flora*).

DRAGM, DRACHMA: dram or drachm: see WEIGHTS AND MEASURES.

ELDER VINEGAR: wine vinegar that has dried elder flowers steeped in it, left to mature in the sun or by the fire (see receipt in John Nott).

ERINGO: sea holly (*Eryngium maritimum*), enjoyed primarily for its candied roots which, as Evelyn noted in his diary (see introduction), were a speciality of Colchester, and esteemed an aphrodisiac.

FARCE: stuffing.

FILLETTING, FILLITING: tape for binding collars and other joints of meat.

FIRKIN: a small barrel, whose size depends on the commodity stored. The ale firkin is 8 gallons: half a kilderkin, or a quarter of a barrel, but Receipts 3 and 4 show beers being made in firkins of varying sizes.

FLITTING DISH: a broad dish used to lift cream off the milk, the word flitting deriving from fleet: to skim.

FLORENTINE, FLORENDINE: a covered tart or pie, often of meat, made with puff paste, which was itself often connected by seventeenth-century cooks with the town of Florence. Karen Hess observes that many early florentines, even those of meat, contained a custard filling. The French equivalent is a *tourte*; the Italian, a *torta*.

GALLENDINE: galantine, but meaning, as in Robert May, q.v., a deep red sauce, not the more familiar cold, jellied meat confection.

GALLY POTT: glazed earthenware pots.

GINNEY BEANES: presumably this refers to beans from the New World, *Phaseolus spp.*

GREATTS: groats.

GROSS, GROSSE, PEPPER: coarsely ground or cracked peppercorns.

GUM DRAGON, GUM DRAGON WATER: gum tragacanth, obtained from the shrub *Astralagus* and used to stabilize, thicken and emulsify. Thought inferior to gum arabic, and used for laundry work. (Glossary to Robert May)

GUTTS: puddings, for instance the liver pudding described in Receipt 41, were often boiled in intestines or guts rather than pudding bags. Robert May suggests that marrow puddings, when done in this way, should be toasted before the fire after boiling. John Nott explains how to fill the guts using a funnel.

HACK: to chop in pieces.

HARSH: hash.

HARTICHOCKE, HARTIC: artichoke.

HARTSHORN: the shavings of a stag's antlers were used to set a jelly. In Receipt 194 it is combined with isinglass (see below), a material that eventually superseded hartshorn in most cookery operations.

HAUTGOUT, HAUTGOUST: when applied to foods, it means properly, even strongly, seasoned, and is often found next to, or in relation to, discussion of French or foreign dishes. Already, by the end of the seventeenth century, it was being used to denote 'high' in the sense that game is high (*OED*). In *Acetaria*, Evelyn also uses the word to denote a gourmet or man well versed in the art of cookery.

HIPPOCRATIC SLEEVE: a bag for straining, said to resemble Hippocrates' sleeve, and 'more probably shaped like the gown-sleeve of a medieval medical man' (C. Anne Wilson). Hippocras, the sweet and spiced red wine, took its name from this implement. The wine was passed through the sleeve, which contained the spices, and absorbed their flavours during transit. One or more passes would be made to vary the degree of absorption before consumption. See D. Hartley, *Water in England*, p. 205 for commentary and illustration.

HOOP: wooden hoop or ring, used when baking cakes in the oven. Receipt 205 makes clear that the hoop was in some instances buttered, and there was a bottom paper, also buttered, to protect the tender cake mixture from the heat of the oven floor. The paper was sometimes a tin sheet. Receipt 207 suggests the cake maker might want to use a 'panne' or a 'hoope'. Receipt 322 contains more instructions about varying the size of a hoop to fit the style of cake being baked, and attaching the hoop to the insulating papers on the bottom.

ISINGLASS: a pure form of commercial gelatine obtained from the swimming bladder or sound of several species of fish, notably the sturgeon. It is well described by Elizabeth David in her glossary to John Nott. The usual manner of its sale, she asserts, was in fine shreds, easily dissolved in water. She suggests that an ounce of isinglass will make a pint and a quarter of water a 'tremulous jelly'. In Receipt 194 its virtues are combined with those of hartshorn, and the compiler notes that Venice isinglass should be obtained. The *Encyclopaedia Britannica* (11th edn.) has a useful article detailing the varieties available at the end of the last century (which did not include 'Venice isinglass'). Isinglass is used today in fining wine.

JELLY BAG: Receipt 195 refers to a flannel bag; Receipt 209 to a double bag.

JORDAN ALMONDS: not from Jordan, but deriving from the word *jardin*, i.e. cultivated, large almonds, normally supplied from Spain.

JULY FLOWER, JULYFLOWER: see CLOVE JULY FLOWER.

KETLE: kettle. An open metal pot used to boil food. The word is still current with this meaning in North American cookery.

KILDERKIN: 16 gallons of beer.

KNEADING TROUGH: the wooden trough designed for kneading and maturing of bread dough is shown in Dorothy Hartley's *Food in England,* p. 499. Receipt 11 has a cake, not bread, being prepared in the trough, though the compiler registers that it may, in this instance, be a pan (presumably of earthenware – a crock). Wooden troughs were not invariably free-standing. Many were smaller, table-top versions, hewn out of a single large chunk of wood.

LADE, LADY: a noun and verb. The verb lade, in Receipt 172 written 'ladying', means to draw water or to empty by 'lading', with a lade or ladle (*OED*). *OED* cites more uses relating to brewing than anything else, although one eighteenth-century book on dairying uses it in the same manner as Evelyn.

LAMBSTONES: lambs' testicles.

LAWNE SIEVE, SIV: a sieve with lawn or fine linen as the mesh.

LEACH: usually called leach of cream in the sixteenth and seventeenth centuries. A leach was a set hard enough to be sliced, the word leach itself originally meaning slice. White leaches were usually made with almonds, but there were some recipes, as Receipt 215, that omitted this ingredient. See Hess for some useful observations.

MARMALADE: a fruit conserve, originally of quinces, made much stiffer than today, thus justifying Evelyn's comment in Receipt 18.

MARROW: invariably bone marrow, not the vegetable.

MEATH: mead. Small meath (Receipt 203) was weaker, just as small beer was the weaker of beers.

MELT, MILT: the soft roe of the male fish, therefore the 'fine melt carpe' in Receipt 23, is the same as Robert May's 'special male carp' (*Accomplisht Cook*, p. 301).

MICHAELMAS: 29th September or, more generally, autumn.

MUSK: the perfume extracted from a gland (the size of an orange) in the male musk-deer, filled with a dark brown or chocolate-coloured secretion which is the consistence of 'moist gingerbread' when fresh, but dries to a granular texture after keeping (*Encyclopaedia Britannica*, 11th edition). Much used in cookery, see Receipt 37 for example, although Karen Hess argues that by the time this MS was compiled both musk and ambergris were out of fashion and more honoured in the breach than the observance of the recipes wherein they figured..

NAPLES BISKETS: Naples biscuits, sponge fingers. In Receipt 162, the compiler refers to 'a role of napell bisket' cut in thin slices. This may imply that 'Naples biscuit' sometimes described the sponge mixture, made into whatever shape was most convenient, rather than the fingers themselves as we now buy or make. Although *A Queens Delight* suggests that Naples biscuit is the same as macaroon mixture, with the addition of pineapple seeds, there is a recipe in John Nott that may fairly be said to represent the norm: 'take a Pound and half of fine Flour, and as much double-refin'd Sugar, twelve Eggs, three Spoonfuls of Rose-water, and an Ounce and half of Carraway-seeds finely pownded, mix them all well together with Water; then put them into Tin-plates, and bake them in a moderate Oven, dissolve some Sugar in Water, and glaze them over.' See also Receipts 244 and 332 for Evelyn's own recipes. As support for the view of *A Queens Delight*, however, note the recommendation of Receipt 40, reiterated in Receipt 41, that the cook should 'grate in two or three maqueroons or Naples biscuits without seeds' when preparing a pudding of entrails.

NEAT: OX.

OLIO, OGLIO: a generic term for a stew, derived from the Spanish *olla (podrida)*, a spiced stew of various meats and vegetables. Note the remarks on olios in *The Compleat Cook* (pp.92–3): 'I am utterly against those confused Olios, into which men put almost all kinds of meats and Roots'.

ONIONS, ONYONS: although the usual form of onion is the one most often referred to, there are also 'green onions', presumably spring onions, young onions, or scallions. Receipt 183 talks of using the blades of young onions, as we would use the tops of spring onions. There is also one reference to 'small green skallions', and a handful to shallots. It may be significant that three of the four uses of shallot are found in recipes of decidedly French influence.

OVEN: the ovens in this text are brick or stone, where the fuel is burnt on the oven floor to heat the fabric, the ashes are raked out, the food substituted for the fire, and cooked with a door tight closed. There are many references to the desired heat of the oven: 'for bread', 'for manchet', 'for pigeon pye', and so forth. In Receipt 172 there is a recommendation that the oven should be heated with one faggot only (the usual, but not inevitable fuel), with some directions about the length of time a faggot takes to burn; in another, there is instruction on how to tell the correct temperature of the oven. The ovens were used for much more than just bread, but it was always slightly trial and error to attain the right heat: experience would be the steadiest guide. See Tom Jaine, *Building a Wood-fired Oven for Bread and Pizza* (1996) for more information.

P, P.: an abbreviation for 'pound'. The full extension, within square brackets (e.g. p[ound]), has usually been inserted into this transcription.

PAPER: kitchen paper was bought in great quantities by the seventeenth- and eighteenth-century cook. Receipt 210 mentions 'halfe brown' paper. Receipt

322 seems to indicate how several thicknesses were used to protect a cake from both bottom and top heat in the oven, as well as discussing the creation of a flow-proof baking vessel out of paper and a wooden baking hoop so that the cake batter would not leak during the initial stages of cooking. Receipt 46 specifies 'clean white paper' with which the cook wraps up some hard lard, placing the parcel on a fork and lighting the paper – the burning fat bastes the roasting turkey and plumps up the flesh.

PARBOIL: to boil thoroughly, or to part-boil. The two opposing meanings were concurrent in the early modern period, although the first was the original. The second, which seems to have gained acceptance merely because it sounded like 'part-boil' and has no philological basis,became the more common usage. The examples in *OED* are ambiguous: it is difficult to be certain what is meant. In Receipt 69 Evelyn states that neats' tongues should be 'half boiled'.

PARMIZAN: Parmesan cheese. In Receipt 7, Evelyn describes it as 'most rare'. Pepys buried his cheese, along with his wine, during the Great Fire of London Evelyn was impressed enough by it during his travels in Italy to mention it twice. In Receipt 15 he suggests a method of preserving it in oil.

PAST: pastry; but it may also mean a paste. A variety of types of pastry are called for, see the index. See also COFFINS.

PATTY PANS: see Receipt 185 where they are called 'potipan moules'. Patt pans were tin moulds such as we might use for small tarts. See, for example, the entries relating to 'Princess Patty Pans' in the York Castle Museum *Kitchen Catalogue*.Other references envisage larger items. Receipt 263, has a patty pan that is thought middle-sized when it takes a pastry crust made with a pound and a half of flour. The summer squash called the pattypan was christened by American settlers, presumably because of its flat, round shape.

PECK: a dry measure, equivalent to a quarter of a bushel, or two gallons. As a measure of weight, 14 pounds. See also WEIGHTS AND MEASURES.

PENNYROYALL: pennyroyal (*Mentha pulegium*), a small-leaved mint.

PILL: peel

PIPKIN: a round pot. Elizabeth David, in her glossary to John Nott, states that such a pot is usually handled. In the main, it was earthenware, although the word might refer to a metal pan. In Receipt 67, Evelyn advises 'a new or very cleane pipkin', which could imply earthenware. Though the sound of pipkin is diminutive, the vessel could be large. A 'great pipkin' was used to make the Spanish olio in Receipt 90. It needed to contain 4 lbs beef, a piece of bacon and pork, neck of mutton, knuckle of veal, a pullet and a couple of pigeons, besides the broth. There are frequent signs of care in the selection of pans, to save food from being tainted for instance. Thus, when making the jelly described in Receipt 67, having boiled up the stock in a new pipkin, it was then strained into an earthen dish.

PISTACCIO: pistachio nut.

POLYPOD: 'polypody of the oak, a common fern growing in sheltered places, old walls, roots and stumps of trees' (E. David, glossary to John Nott). The root was used in medicine (see also Sir Kenelm Digby).

POMATE: mash.

PORRINGER, PORRENGER: a bowl used for eating. *The Compleat Cook* (p.93) comments that he would rather a broth was 'drunk out of a Porringer, than … eaten with a spoon.' The word is still current in Scotland to describe a bowl for eating porridge.

POSSETT, POSSETT POTT: possetts were drinks made with hot milk curdled with wine or other liquor, together with various flavourings. They were made by heating alcohol in one bowl or pan and the milk or cream in another, then pouring the milk into the liquor from a great height. This was left to froth up and separate outby the side of the fire before drinking. The possett pot in such a production would presumably be the bowl in which the possett reposed, rather than the brass saucepan used to boil up the milk. See also SYLLABUB.

POSTLE: this word is used by Evelyn, in Receipt 68, to describe the sinewy part of the leg of venison. The derivation of the word is unknown. Postil or postle means a marginal comment (*OED*).

POTTLE, POTLE, POTTELL: half a gallon (*SOED*).See WEIGHTS AND MEASURES.

POWDER: to powder meat, i.e. to dry cure it with salt or spices. This was done in powdering tubs, a frequent item in inventories of early kitchens.

PUFFS: although puff often meant a light form of bread, and was used to describe light, butter-filled pastry, it was also two sorts of generic dish of which several examples exist in this manuscript. There were curd-based puffs mixed with flour and shaped then usually fried like fritters, and cream-based boiled puff puddings.

Q.S., QUA: S:, Q.SS.: *quantum sufficit*, as much as is sufficient; see also WEIGHTS AND MEASURES.

QUARTERNE: a quarter of anything. Its use in Receipt 16 is ambiguous, it may mean a quarter of a pound. In Receipt 84, he talks of 'a quarterne and a half' of butter, which presumably means either three-quarters of a pound or six ounces. There are also instructions to take 'half a quarter', which must indicate two ounces. (See WEIGHTS AND MEASURES.)

R.: abbreviation for *Recipe* (from the Latin: the imperative form of *recipere*, to receive), or its English equivalent, 'Take', often placed at the outset of instructions.

RACE: root (of ginger).

RAISINS, REASONS: sun-dried grapes, sometimes called raisins-of-the-sun to distinguish them from raisins of Corinth, i.e. currants. In Receipt 105, they are called 'malago raisins'.

RAPE VINEGAR: vinegar made from the stalks of grape clusters, or refuse of grapes from which wine has been expressed (*OED*).

RED DOCK: *Rumex*. In *Acetaria*, Evelyn recommends using the roots of the sharp-pointed dock for brewing.

ROCCOMBO: rocambole (*Allium scorodoprasum*).

RUNDLET, RUNDLETT: runlet. A cask or barrel – small runlets contained between a 'pint and a quart and 3 or 4 gallons' (*SOED*).

SACK, SACKE: white Spanish or Canary wine. Gervase Markham wrote (cited in *OED*), 'Your best Sacks are of Seres in Spaine, your smaller from Galicia and Portugall; your strong Sacks are of the Islands of Canaries, and of Malligo.' The MS qualifies the word in Receipt 126 where it calls for 'best malago', and Receipt 209 where the need is for Canary. Receipt 54 called for 'sacke or other strong wine' indicating that these wines were fortified in the manner of sherry. Sherry is denoted once in these receipts (243).

SALL PRUNELLA: salprunella. If saltpetre (nitre) is fixed by burning with charcoal, it becomes salprunella: a nitrite instead of a nitrate (see glossary to Hannah Glasse). It colours pickled meats.

SALT: there were different sorts of salt available, see Elizabeth David, *Spices, Salts and Aromatics in the English Kitchen* (1970), and the glossary to Hannah Glasse for some discussion:
> BAY SALT: salt made from the evaporation of seawater in salt pans by the natural heat of the sun. This was usually imported from the hotter climes of southern Europe.

> WHITE SALT: salt made by the evaporation of seawater and brine (for instance from the brine springs of Cheshire) by artificially heating it.

SALTPETRE: potassium or sodium nitrate.

SAMPHIER, SAMPIER: rock samphire (*Crithmum maritimum*), rather than the marsh samphire with which it is often confused.

SANDERS, RED SANDERS: a dye obtained from the red sandalwood tree.

SAUCEPAN: Receipt 317 specifies that the saucepan or stewpan be tinned when potting pigeons.

SAXAFRAS: sassafras, a tree native to Florida. The bark was used in medicine and to make a calming tea (E. David, glossary to John Nott).

SCEMING DISH: skimming dish. A flat, perforated brass skimmer. These were used in the production of clotted cream, among other things, but Evelyn also noted the use of a flat wooden trencher to skim the cream off the milk in Normandy (Receipt 100).Receipt 172 also calls for a wooden trencher in making a 'clouted cream'.

SCOTCH: to score a piece of meat or fish with the tip of a knife, nothing to do with Scotland. The word scarify is used in Receipt 125 for eels, for roughly the same act.

SCRAPED SUGAR: scraped with a knife off the block, which was the form it entered the household, rather than the powdered sugar we have today.

SCURVY-GRASS, SCURVY GRASSE: *Cochlearia officinalis.*

SEAME, SEAM: fat or grease.

SEARCE, SEARSE, SERSE: to sift or sieve.

SERVICE: a self-contained stage in a meal, or an individual dish. In Receipt 185 the patties or pasties can either act as garnish or, if they are made with puff paste, 'they are a service by themselves served alltogether in a dish.' Meals originally consisted of one or more services of several dishes, of contrasting, opposing or complementary flavours.The MS uses the word in both its accepted senses.The words service and course may be interchangeable. Receipt 21 has venison served at the second course; Receipt 37 is for a lobster pie for the second service. Receipt 301 talks of sending stewed apples 'in with the dessert'. Charles Carter's *The Complete Practical Cook* (1730) has many plans of dinner tables which reflect usage at the end of Evelyn's life.

SHALLOTS: see ONIONS.

SIMPER: simmer.

SIPPETT: slices or small triangles of fried, dried or toasted bread, or sometimes puff pastry, used to ornament a dish. In Receipt 91 they should be of manchet 'roasted crispe by a quick fire'. The word is the diminutive of sop, also used by Evelyn, e.g. in Receipt 72. See Karen Hess, p. 40, for a short discussion. Receipt 8 seems to imply that sippetts are creatures of fashion: 'the Sippetts now in use wherewith this must be served…'.

SIV: sieve

SKILLET, SKELLET: a metal cooking pot, often with legs to stand in the fire, cast in one piece.

SKERRIT, SKARRETT: skirret (*Sium sisarum*), a species of water parsnip cultivated for its root.

SMALL EDGE: smallage (*Apium graveolens*), wild or primitive celery.

SODDE, SOD: boiled.

SOPPS: see SIPPETTS

SOUCE, SOUSE, sowce: a pickling liquid, often referred to as a 'sousing drink'; also a verb, meaning to pickle or to immerse in a pickle.

STAMPE, STAMP: crush, grind.

STROAKINGS: the milk that is taken from the cow when stripping the udder at the end of milking. It is richer than other milk. It was sometimes called afterings. In *The Compleat Cook* (p. 78), it says, 'Take a gallon of Stroakings, and a pint of Cream as it comes from the Cow, and put it together with a little Rennet,' in order to make angelot cheese.

SUCCORY: chicory (*Cichorium intybus*).

SUGAR: There were many sorts of sugar at this period. See the entry in the glossary to Hannah Glasse. C. Anne Wilson's *Food and Drink in Britain* is useful on the types of sugar available in the seventeenth century. See also the glossary to Richard Bradley.

DOUBLE REFINED SUGAR: sugar was refined in the country of origin but this was often insufficient for European taste, so local refineries were established that produced the white loaves of sugar familiar from contemporary still-lifes. Double refined sugar is therefore particularly white.

LOAF SUGAR: describes the conical form in which sugar was produced after its refinement in England or Europe. A discussion and illustration are to be found in Elizabeth David, *English Bread and Yeast Cookery*, 1977. Where the recipe calls for sugar to be 'beat', this refers to the fact that most sugar entered the household in loaf form. After detaching lumps with cutters designed for the purpose, they have still to be ground in a mortar, or through a sieve, into usable powder.Sometimes a recipe calls for sugar to be 'grossly' beaten, others for it to be finer.

TREBLE REFINED SUGAR: mentioned in Receipt 156 is even whiter. It is sometimes called royal sugar.

SYLLABUB: there are several recipes for syllabub (for instance numbers 175, 216 and 217) which speak of various bits of equipment for this dish – see WOODEN COW, below, for one of them – and a variety of techniques for making it curdle or to whip up a foam. The accepted way that milk should be added to a syllabub is seen in the near invariable use of the phrase, 'milk the milk to…'. Receipt 139 calls for the cream to be poured into the syllabub pot through a funnel from on high. Receipt 265 repeats this instruction, and adds a rider emphasising the need to pour the cream from a high spot to make it 'curdle the better'. Some syllabub glasses had spouts on them to draw or drink off the whey from the curds; others were simply glass bowls in which the syllabub could be mixed without tainting the milk; still more seem to be churns or stoppered glass vessels (for instance, that mentioned by Elinor Fettiplace).

TAFFATA TART: taffeta was a word applied to a cream dish, taffeta cream, and to a tart. The two coexist in John Nott's *Cooks Dictionary*. Elizabeth David, who compiled the glossary for the 1980 facsimile of that work, suggested the creams were so called because their lustrous surface matched the sheen of taffeta silk. However, she was unable to make the link between a simple egg cream and (in the case of John Nott) a tart of high-flavoured apple purée. The *OED* connects the word in its culinary sense with the figurative usage, for example Shakespeare's 'taffata phrases, silken tearmes precise', when it means bombastic, florid, highly decorated.

TAMARIS: leaves of the tamarisk tree were used in medicinal decoctions and, in Receipt 128, in ale which was in fact described as 'medicinal'.

TANSY: a flat omelette, sometimes thickened with crumbs, and coloured green with juice of vegetables and herbs (tansy). Variations, like apple, also exist.

THISTLE: in Receipt 78[bis] for a thistle salad, Evelyn may be referring to the cardoon, although when this recipe reappeared in *Acetaria* he changed his introductory description from 'the great thistle' to 'the milky thistle'. In a letter printed in Bray (Wheatley), volume III (p. 359), Evelyn tells the Earl of Sandwich, then ambassador at Madrid, that 'I think I was the first that ever planted Spanish Cardôns in our country for any culinarie use, as y^r Ex^{cy}: has taught the blanching; but I know not whether they serve themselves in Spaine with the purple beards of the thistle, when it is in flower, for the curdling of milk, which it performes much better than reinet, and is far sweeter in the dairy than that liquor, which is apt to putrifie.'

TIFFANIE, TIFFANY: fine silk or lawn used as a mesh for sieving and straining, or as cloth to make up a spice bag.

TREADS, TREDS: see COCK TREADINGS.

TRENCHER: a piece of stale bread cut from a large oblong loaf (see Karen Hess) used as a plate in the medieval and early modern period. The word derives from the French *trancher* (to slice, cut or hack) and indicated at root the surface upon which meat or food was sliced or cut. The bread trencher is thus a specialised form and in fact any flat board or plate used for this purpose could be called a trencher. By extension, the term was used for flat boards, for cutting or not. In Receipt 100, Evelyn describes a wooden trencher, held on the thumb like a painter's palette, used to skim cream off milk. Here, he is recalling a French method of working, but in Receipt 172 he is using the instrument in an English kitchen: 'a wooden trencher made round and thin'. In Receipt 68, a weighted trencher is placed on top of a joint of potted venison to hold it below the surface of the butter that will preserve it. Again, this would have been a flat wooden or metal platter, not a piece of dry bread. See also SCEMING DISH.

UNCIA: an ounce, often expressed by a symbol in the MS, but printed in this transcript in full . One twelfth of a pound troy. An ounce avoirdupois is 437 grains, an ounce troy 480 grains. (See WEIGHTS AND MEASURES.)

VERJUICE, VERDJUICE: sour juice from unripe grapes or crab apples.

VITRIOL: spirit of vitriol is the distilled essence of vitriol – sulphuric acid (OED). This authority also quotes the *Encyclopaedia Britannica*, 1771, which states, 'if the vitriolic acid contain much water', it is spirit of vitriol. Its taste was both acid and salty. Receipt 217 uses it by the drop.

WAFFERS, WAFER: wafers, waffles, *gaufres*: crisp honeycombed pancakes ('hollow biscuits', Receipt 210) made in a wafer iron. See the index for mentions of this implement in the text, and note the instructions for ways of greasing and handling it.

WALME, WALM: the heaving action of boiling.

WATER: many of the receipts specify the type of water to be used, or at the least insist it should be 'fair' water, which in this context means pure. Compare Dorothy Hartley's comments in her *Water in England*, and Hilary Spurling's in her edition of Elinor Fettiplace. Receipt 62 uses fountain water to mix an orange drink; Receipt 67, for jelly of veal, demands fair conduit water, while 243, for calves foot jelly, says spring water; Receipt 145, for collar of beef, suggests the hardest pump water obtainable; and Receipt 186, for currant wine, advises spring water. Alan Davidson wrote an entertaining piece about Thom. Cocke's *Kitchin Physick* (1676) in *Twelve Times a Year*, March 1985, which is a book that puts water (and watergruel, see for instance Evelyn's Receipt 30) in perspective.

WEIGHTS AND MEASURES: many of the words used to denote size, weight or volume in this manuscript are given their own entry in this glossary.

However, the first page of the original volume containing these receipts is an ornamental title page, headed 'RECEIPTS MEDICINAL'. It contains tables of weights and measures, and notes of the symbols used for minerals, aspects and astrological signs. The weights and measures defined are as follows:

'GENERAL: Granum or a Barley Corne out of the midst of ye Eare; Scrupulus a Scruple or 20 Barley Cornes; obolus or 10 Gr.; Drachma or 3 Scruples; Uncia or 8 Dragmes; Libra or a Pound containing 12 oz.; Manipulus or a great handfull; Pugillum or a small handfull; Aña, of each alike; q.s., quantum sufficit, as much as is sufficient.

[This set of measurements is based on the troy pound of 12 ounces or 5,760 grains, used by apothecaries and in bullion transactions. The avoirdupois pound was 7,000 grains and 16 ounces and was used in markets and everyday kitchens. The presumption has to be that most of the culinary receipts, as opposed to those for medicines, or perhaps still-room concoctions, used avoirdupois. Note, however, that the measures employed in Receipt 2 are troy ounces of 8 drams, not the avoirdupois ounce of 16 drams. It is most likely that the Evelyn kitchen did not own weights for the ounce avoirdupois, only the ounce troy. There are several instructions, for example in Receipt 80, to take 'half a quarter', where we would have written '2 ounces'.]

'THE MEASURE OF LIQUIDS: A Pinte; a Quart is two pints; a Pottell is two Quarts; a Gallon is two Pottells.

'THE MEASURE OF ARIDS: A Pecke is 2 Gallons; a Bushell 4 Peckes; a Coumb 4 Bushells; a Quarter 2 Coumbs.

'ALE MEASURE: Ale measure to wine measure is in proportion as 33 to 28, or in lesse terms is 16 1/2 to 14. Therefore one quart of Ale should conteine one quart, & 7 tenths of a quart so that if the ale q^{rt} conteine 2 wine q^{rts} it is too great by 3 tenths of a quart. The surest way therefore will be by weight, for a true ale quart must conteyne in water 2 pound 6 ounces.'

WHISK: although there are suggestions that eggs and similar substances should be whisked with a piece of wood split into four (for instance Receipts 132 and

168), there is also (Receipt 210) a mention of the action of whisking with no comment on the tool itself. John Nott, in his recipe for Snow Cream, suggests that the cook rolls a cleft stick between his or her hands to effect the whisking motion, and *The Compleat Cook* advises you to roll between your hands a whisk made of a bundle of reeds tied together. Receipt 32 specifies a whisk of dry birch twigs, with a bunch of rosemary and a sliver of lemon peel tied into the bundle to impart their special fragrances to a whipped cream.

WHITPOTT: whitepot: a custard or milk pudding, mainly in Devonshire (*OED*).

WINE QUART: a measure – one quarter of a wine gallon, the equivalent of the US gallon, smaller than the imperial gallon. (See WEIGHTS AND MEASURES.)

WOODEN COW: some syllabubs were made by drawing the milk directly from the cow on to alcohol and/or acids. If you lacked a cow, you could replicate the effect as Sir Kenelm Digby advises in his receipt: 'Take a reasonable quantity (as about half a Porrenger full) of the Syrup, that hath served in the making of dryed plums; and into a large Syllabub-pot milk or squirt, or let fall from high a suficient quantity of Milk or Cream.' To achieve the 'squirt', an instrument, presumably like a syringe, was available. It was called a wooden cow. In one of John Nott's recipes for syllabub he recommends you to 'squirt them into the Pot with a wooden Cow made for the Purpose, which you may buy at the Turners.' The cow is suggested in the Evelyn MS as an aid to making buttermilk curds, Receipt 158. See also C. Anne Wilson, pp. 170–1.

YEST: yeast. Yeast was not then supplied in dried cake form, nor did it derive, as now, from molasses or distillers' activities. Rather was it ale yeast, often barm, the froth taken off the top of a fermenting vat of ale, hence the large measures required – pints or more – to leaven a particular batch of dough. Evelyn and his fellow compilers do not refer to barm, only to yeast. If a quantity of barm is left standing, the yeasts will fall as sediment. This can then be extracted, washed or diluted and used as a liquid or a semi-solid. See Elizabeth David, *English Bread and Yeast Cookery* for more information. Receipt 322 is more specific: 'the yest must be neither bitter nor thin nor with the drink but indifferent thick and light.'

A view of Wotton in the Georgian period. The original house, occupied by
John Evelyn, has vanished, although the wing on the left-hand side dates from
that era. Today, much of the exterior is a Victorian jacobethan pastiche. The
gardens, and John Evelyn's precious woods, have survived to a remarkable
degree, even if the view presented here is more redolent of Brown or Repton.

Index

This index includes most substantive references to dishes and to ingredients in the receipts. Exceptions are sugar, cream, eggs, flour, salt, pepper, and bread, unless they are distinguished in some way from the ordinary. Kitchen implements have also been indexed, though excepting bowls, dishes, etc., unless, again, they are in some way distinguished within the text itself. Spelling has been modernized, with only a tithe of the variations in the text being signalled. Most references are to receipt numbers, not to pages. Page references (for the introduction and glossary) are prefixed by p.

References without prefix are to receipt numbers; page references are prefixed p.

References without prefix are to receipt numbers; page references are prefixed p.

References without prefix are to receipt numbers; page references are prefixed p.

References without prefix are to receipt numbers; page references are prefixed p.

References without prefix are to receipt numbers; page references are prefixed p.